BEING
MENTALLY
ILL

OBSERVATIONS

A series edited by Howard S. Becker
Northwestern University

BEING
MENTALLY
ILL

A Sociological Theory

BY THOMAS J. SCHEFF

Aldine • Atherton | Chicago • New York

First published 1966 by
ALDINE Publishing Company
529 South Wabash Avenue
Chicago, Illinois 60605

ISBN 0-202-30002-1, Cloth;
      0-202-30252-0, Paper.

Library of Congress Catalog Card Number 66-15207
Designed by David Miller
Printed in the United States of America

Second printing, 1967
Third printing, 1968
Fourth printing, 1970
Fifth printing, 1971
First Paperbound Edition, 1971

Fernando Romero, chief of one of Mexico City's secret police corps, was attacked by a demented opponent in a hall near his office late Friday night. The attacker raised a razor against Romero when the latter opened the door to the hall. Romero immediately closed the door and called for his aides. The man was disarmed and brought to Romero who, realizing the man was insane, admonished him and sent him home. México (D. F.) News

No point in cluttering up an asylum with a lot of nuts. The New Yorker, *May 15, 1965.*

We have endeavored . . . to observe a kind of perspective, that one part may cast light upon another. Francis Bacon, Advancement of Learning

Acknowledgments

SUPPORT for the writing of this book was provided by the following: the Graduate Research Committee of the University of California, Santa Barbara; the Social Science Research Council; and the Center for the Study of Law and Society, University of California, Berkeley.

Parts of the text have appeared earlier as articles: "The Social Role of the Mentally Ill and the Dynamics of Mental Disorder: A Research Framework," *Sociometry,* 26 (December, 1963), pp. 436-453 (parts of Chapters 2 and 3); "Social Supports for Stereotypes of Mental Illness," *Mental Hygiene,* 47 (July, 1963), pp. 461-469 (part of Chapter 3); "Decision Rules, Types of Error, and their Consequences in Medical Diagnosis," *Behavioral Science,* 8 (April, 1963), pp. 97-107 (part of Chapter 4); "The Societal Reaction to Deviance: Ascriptive Elements in the Psychiatric Screening of Mental Patients in a Midwestern State," *Social Problems,* 11 (Spring, 1964), pp. 401-413 (Study 1 in Chapter 5). Some of the data presented in Study II, Chapter 5, were described in "Legitimate, Transitional, and Illegitimate Mental Patients in a Midwestern State," *American Journal of Psychiatry,* 120 (September, 1963), pp. 267-269; and "Typification in Diagnosis," *Sociology and Rehabilitation* (in press), contains part of Chapter 5. Permission to republish these articles in revised form is gratefully acknowledged to these journals.

I wish to acknowledge the help of the following persons: Sarah Bradly composed and drew the montage and flow chart in Chapter 3; Walter Buckley gave helpful advice on theory and systems; Howard Becker, Arlene Daniels and Tamotsu Shibutani read earlier drafts and gave editorial advice; Arlene Daniels also proofread the final draft. Needless to say, the errors and inconsistencies in this book are entirely my responsibility.

Contents

BEING
MENTALLY
ILL

THE purpose of this book is the formulation of a
sociological theory that is relevant to the understanding
of the condition known as "chronic mental illness." The
discussion assumes some familiarity with sociological
vocabulary, and acquaintance with two somewhat separate fields: psychiatric classifications of behavior patterns, on the one hand, and the sociology of deviant
behavior, on the other. For the reader who desires supplementary information in these areas, the following
remarks may be helpful.

For a text that gives a good description of the commonly accepted psychiatric syndromes, yet also conveys
some of the perplexing ambiguities in psychiatric classifications and theories, see N. H. Pronko, *Textbook of
Abnormal Psychology* (Baltimore: Williams and Wilkins,
1963). Any textbook in psychiatry or abnormal psychology
would prove useful, however.

For the reader unfamiliar with sociological terms,
six central concepts are briefly defined in the text: norm,
rule-breaking, deviance, role, career, and status. The
definitions of *norm, rule-breaking,* and *deviance* are
found on pages 31-33 of Chapter 2. Social *role* is defined
in footnote 3, Chapter 3, *career* in footnote 36, Chapter
3, and *status* in footnote 2, Chapter 5. For a fuller discussion of the major sociological concepts, the reader

1

is referred to an introductory text in sociology, such as L. Broom and P. Selznick, *Sociology* (New York: Harper and Row, 1963). For supplementary reading in the sociology of deviance, see Howard Becker, *Outsiders* (New York: The Free Press of Glencoe, 1963).

It is important that the reader avoid the conclusion that the use of these six concepts involves merely quibbling over the choice of terms, and that the use of the associated common sense terms would do just as well. Why should we replace the term abnormal with deviant, or mental illness with residual deviance? The answer to this question is that implicit in such terms as "abnormal" and "mental illness" is an entire theory of behavior, complete with unstated, and usually unconsidered concepts, assumptions, and propositions about the nature of man, human relationships, and society. To get a fresh look at the problem of mental disorder, the discussion is conducted in a language that is not based on the assumptions that are currently conventional.

The clearest example of the importance of the implications of terms is provided by the contrast between the common-sense meaning of the word "deviant," and the special sociological sense in which it is used here. In ordinary usage, deviant is applied to something which is inherently undesirable. The word has the strong connotation of badness, evil, moral wrong. As explained below, however, when the word is used in this discussion, the author is *not* expressing his own evaluation of the behavior as good or bad, desirable or undesirable, but is merely reporting the evaluation made by society. The frame of reference is not morally absolute, but relative to the standards and specific reactions of whatever society is under discussion. To be sure, this tactic does not solve the host of vexing moral problems that are found in the area of mental illness, but merely bypasses them. It bypasses them, not because they are unimportant, but because the purpose of this particular approach is to attempt to describe how people act, rather than how they should act. That is, the purpose of the proposed theory is a specialized one, the specification of regularities in human behavior. I hope that this purpose will help to justify the unconventional and sometimes awkward terminology in the text that follows.

PART
I

Theory

I

Theory

1

Introduction:
Individual and Social Systems
in Deviance

ALTHOUGH the last five decades have seen a vast number of studies of functional mental disorder, there is as yet no substantial, verified body of knowledge in this area. At this writing there is no rigorous knowledge of the cause, cure, or even the symptoms of functional mental disorders. Such knowledge as there is, is clinical and intuitive, and thus not subject to verification by scientific methods.

Consider, for example, the research which has been done on the origins of schizophrenia, one of the major mental disorders. Lewis reports that from 1920 to 1934, 1,778 papers, monographs and books were published on organic studies of schizophrenia.[1] For the period from 1935 to 1945, Bellak counted 3,200 studies on this subject.[2] Finally, for the period 1940 to 1960, Jackson counted some 500 papers on etiology alone.[3] Even allowing for the overlap between Bellak's and Jackson's reports, we can estimate that there have been at least five thousand papers reporting research on schizophrenia in the five decades since 1920.

1. N. D. C. Lewis, *Research in Dementia Praecox* (New York: The National Committee for Mental Hygiene, 1936).
2. L. Bellak, *Dementia Praecox: The Past Decade's Work and Present Status: A Review and Evaluation* (New York: Grune and Stratton, 1948).
3. D. D. Jackson, "Introduction," in *The Etiology of Schizophrenia* (New York: Basic Books, 1960), p. 4.

7

What progress has been made as a result of this massive investigation of schizophrenia? Arieti summarizes the results of the organic studies:

> The quantity of these works and the variety of directions which they have taken reveal that no headway has been made and that no constructive avenue of research has yet been found in the organic field.[4]

Jackson, summarizing the later papers, states:

> These papers disagree widely with one another and reflect the fact that schizophrenia is a singularly difficult disorder to investigate . . .
>
> At present, schizophrenia is one of our major medical problems. This is not only because of its incidence (estimated at from one to three per cent of the population) and its chronicity (keeping one quarter of the hospital beds in the country occupied), or because of the fact that its major incidence is during the most productive periods of life, roughly between the ages of 15 and 44. *It is also because medicine has made progress against many other major disorders, thus allowing schizophrenia to loom large by contrast.*[5] [emphasis added.]

In other words, Jackson is saying that in research on schizophrenia, virtually no progress has been made.

The enormous outpouring of time and effort in the study of schizophrenia, and the insignificant findings from this effort, have caused considerable concern among psychiatric researchers. Many of these researchers have suggested that what is needed is not only more research, but research which departs radically from the framework in which these earlier studies were made. A quotation from a recent symposium on schizophrenia suggests the need for a fundamental shift in perspective:

4. S. Arieti, *Interpretation of Schizophrenia* (New York: Robert Brunner, 1955), p. 9.

5. Jackson, *op. cit.*, pp. 3-4.

During the past decade, the problems of chronic schizophrenia have claimed the energy of workers in many fields. Despite significant contributions which reflect continuing progress, *we have yet to learn to ask ourselves the right questions.*[6] [emphasis added.]

Many investigators, not only in the field of schizophrenia, but from all the studies of functional mental disorder, apparently now agree; not only have systematic studies failed to provide answers to the problem of causation, but there is considerable feeling that the problem itself has not been formulated correctly.

One frequently noted deficiency in psychiatric formulations of the problem is the failure to incorporate social processes into the dynamics of mental disorder. Although the importance of these processes is increasingly recognized by psychiatrists, the conceptual models used in formulating research questions are basically concerned with individual rather than social systems. Genetic, biochemical, and psychological investigations seek different causal agents, but utilize similar models: dynamic systems that are located within the individual. In these investigations, social processes tend to be relegated to a subsidiary role, because the model focuses attention on individual differences rather than on the social system in which the individual is involved.

Even in the theories that are not organic in nature, the social system is relegated to a relatively minor place in the understanding of mental illness. This is true in psychoanalytic theory, the most influential of the nonorganic theories, although Freud and his students frequently noted the importance of the social and cultural setting. In order to underscore the importance of the

6. N. S. Apter, "Our Growing Restlessness with Problems of Chronic Schizophrenia," in L. Appleby, *et al., Chronic Schizophrenia* (New York: Free Press, 1960).

system properties of a theory, it is useful to compare psychoanalytic ideas, which are built around individual systems, with Marxist analysis, which is entirely social systemic, and excludes completely any consideration of individual systems.

In psychoanalytic theory, the origins of neurosis are external to the individual. Freud's formulation was: "The Oedipus complex is the kernel of every neurosis." Fenichel, Freud's disciple and chief codifier of psychoanalytic ideas, states:

The Oedipus complex is the normal climax of infantile sexual development as well as the basis of all neuroses.[7]

According to this theory, all children pass through a stage in which the parent of the opposite sex is chosen as a sexual object, causing intense hostility and rivalry toward the parent of the same sex. For children who go on to become normal adults, the Oedipal conflict is resolved: the child rejects the opposite-sex parent as a sexual object and identifies with the parent of his same sex. The rejection of his parent as a sexual object frees him from later incestuous and therefore guilt-laden sexual impulses, and the identification with the same-sex parent begins the formation of the super-ego, which is the very basis for a normal adult psychic structure.

If, however, the opposite-sex parent is not rejected as a sex object, and the same-sex parent not taken as a model, a fundamental fault is created in the psychic structure. In this case, the person grows into an adult who is never psychologically separated from his parents: throughout his life he is fighting and refighting the Oedipal conflict. All his relations with persons of the opposite sex are tinged with incestuous guilt, because

7. O. Fenichel, *The Psychoanalytic Theory of Neurosis* (New York: W. W. Norton, 1945), p. 108.

his perceptions are based on his early childhood images in the family. Similarly, all his relations with same-sex persons are colored by the hostility and rivalry he felt for his parent of the same sex. According to this theory, the boy who goes through childhood without resolving the Oedipal conflict never establishes new relationships with women or men in later life, but is imprisoned within the incestuous, and therefore psychologically untenable, relationship with his mother, and the hostile, rivalry-ridden relationship with his father.

Fenichel notes that the social situation in the child's family at the time of the Oedipal conflict is a key determinant of whether the conflict is resolved. The absence of the one of the parents, or the weakness of one or the other as a model, as well as many other contingencies, are potential causes of lack of resolution. It should be noted, however, that these external sources of defect are no longer involved in the neurotic system of behavior after the Oedipal stage passes (approximately from the ages of three to seven years.) If the Oedipal conflict is not resolved at this stage, the psychic flaw will continue throughout later life, more or less independently of later life experiences. It is true that psychoanalysts do speak of precipitating factors in adult life, but it is clear that these factors are of only subsidiary interest. The person in the throes of the Oedipal conflict is a defective adult, such that stresses that others could easily surmount may plunge him into a full-scale neurosis.

Thus the psychoanalytic model of neurosis is basically a system of behavior that is contained within the individual. The external situation in which the individual is involved is seen only as an almost limitless source of triggers for a fully developed neurotic conflict within the individual. Psychoanalytic theory, like most contemporary theories of mental illness, whether they are psychological or organic, locates the neurotic system within the individual. To be sure, psychoanalysts, like other psychiatric theorists, allow for external causation. Fenichel states:

The normal person has few "troops of occupation" remaining at the position "Oedipus complex," to use Freud's metaphor, the majority of his troops having marched on. However, under *great* duress they, too, may retreat, and thus a normal person may become neurotic. The person with a neurotic disposition has left nearly all his forces at the Oedipus complex; only a few have advanced, and at the slightest difficulty they have to go back and rejoin the main force at their first stand, the Oedipus complex.[8]

Similar disclaimers can be found in virtually all the current theories of mental illness. Needless to say, in these theories, as in psychoanalytic theory, the direction and thrust of the perspective is found not in these exceptions and qualifications, but in systemic linkages that they posit, connecting key characteristics of individuals with their neurotic behavior. In psychoanalytic theory, the great conceptual development occurs in linking the origins of neurosis in the Oedipal stage through the mechanisms of psychosexual development to their end result, which is treated by the psychoanalyst theoreticians in a great wealth of detail: the formations of dreams, everyday slips and errors, and finally, in their manifold variety and complexity, the neurotic symptoms.

Many of the critics of psychoanalytic theory have focused on just this feature as objectionable: the tracing of the most diverse kinds of human reactions back to the generic psychological substructure resulting from the Oedipal conflict. Freud's critics claim that the psychoanalytic model of man is too tight, narrow, rigid, and

8. *Idem.*

one-dimensional. The way in which psychoanalysts have sought to show how artistic creativity derives from psychosexual conflict is a case in point. Critics have also objected to Freud's key postulate of the "overdetermination" of symptoms. The literature of psychoanalysis abounds in instances showing how a symptom is not simply a consequence of a single cause, but is merely one aspect of a veritable network of psychic phenomena. It is for this reason that psychoanalysts are usually adverse to the treatment of symptoms: their theory leads them to expect that if a symptom is removed, without changing the basic psychological structure, a new symptom will shortly appear in its place. But critics have objected that psychoanalytic theory seems to posit a type of predestination, in which the neurotic is prisoner of his inexorable neurotic system.

From the point of view of the construction of a viable scientific theory, however, much of this criticism seems misplaced. It is just the "systemness" of psychoanalytic theory that makes it such a powerful intellectual weapon for the investigation of neurotic behavior. Starting from relatively few general postulates, it develops an enormous number of propositions about very concrete types of behavior. Such a theory is both powerful, in that it ramifies into many areas of behavior, and at least potentially refutable, so that with an adequate program of empirical research it could be qualified, transformed, or rejected.

Furthermore, the notion of the "overdetermination" of symptoms is very much in accord with recent developments in theory construction. In general systems theory, for example, the idea of overdetermination is closely related to the model of a self-maintaining system. The key feature of such a system is "negative feedback," such that deviations from the system's steady state are detected and fed back into the system in such a way as to cause the system to return to its steady state. There is no reason to believe that such a system is found in only biological or electronic realms; psychoanalytic interpretations have suggested many ways in which psychological systems have this property. In the discussion in the following chapters, a system with self-maintaining properties comprising the deviant and those reacting to him will be delineated.

The objection to psychoanalytic theory that is made here is not that it posits neurotic behavior as part of a closed system, but that the system that it formulates is too narrow, in that it leaves out aspects of the social context that are vital for understanding mental disorder. The basic model upon which psychoanalysis is constructed is the disease model, in that it portrays neurotic behavior as unfolding relentlessly out of a defective psychological system that is entirely contained within the body. To bring the individual systemic character of psychoanalytic theory into high relief, it is instructive to contrast it with Marxian theory, which is social systemic.

Like Freud, Marx began his analysis with relatively few, but highly abstract, postulates. Chief among these postulates is the dictum that in any society it is the mode of production that determines the basic social forms, including the economic and political systems, the direction and pace of social change, and, ultimately, even man's consciousness. This point is made very clearly when Marx states that the mode of production is the substructure, and all other forms mere superstructure, in any society. Marx went on to construct from this basic premise a theory of history and of society in which the characteristics of individuals are more or less irrelevant.

In his analysis of then contemporary Europe, Marx posited the accumulation of capital as the process that determined social structure and social change. In primitive capitalism, the critical step was the accumulation of sufficient capital that a man's subsistence was not continually in jeopardy. The early capitalist could afford to bargain for his labor, rather than accept whatever the market offered. Society was transformed into two classes, those in a bargaining position (the capitalists) and those who were not (the workers). In the course of bargaining, the market rates for labor inevitably assumed the bottom limit, the cost of the worker's subsistence, and the capitalists, by the same logic, inevitably waxed rich at the worker's expense. For our purposes, the interesting feature of Marx's theory was the manner in which it disregarded the motivations of the individuals involved. For the capitalists, for example, it did not matter whether they were humanitarian or not, for the development of the capitalist system. A capitalist, who, for humane reasons, refused to expropriate the workers, would himself be expropriated by other capitalists. Marx and his followers felt that they had evolved a theory that was independent of the psychology of individuals.

From these considerations, Marx stated the law of capital accumulation:

But all methods for the production of surplus value are at the same time methods of accumulation; and every extension of accumulation becomes again a means for the development of those methods. It follows therefore that in proportion as capital accumulates, the lot of the laborer, be his payment high or low, must grow worse. The law, finally, that always equilibrates the relative surplus-population, or industrial reserve army, to the extent and energy of accumulation, this law rivets the laborer to capital more firmly than the wedges of Vulcan did Prometheus to the rock. It established an accumulation of misery, corresponding with accumulation of capital. Accumulation of wealth at one pole is, therefore, at the same time accumulation of misery, agony of toil, slavery, ignorance, brutality, and mental degradation, at the other pole.[9]

Marx notes the social and psychological effect of this process on the individual laborer:

Within the capitalist system all methods for raising the social productiveness of labor are brought about at the cost of the individual laborer; all means for the development of production transform themselves into domination over, and exploitation of, the producers; they mutilate the laborer into a fragment of a man, degrade him to the level of an appendage of a machine, destroy every remnant or charm in his work and turn it into a hated toil; they estrange from him the intellectual potentialities of the labor process in the same proportion as science is incorporated in it as an independent power; they distort the conditions under which he works, subject him during the labor process to a despotism the more hateful for its meanness; they transform his life-time to a working time, and drag his wife and child beneath the wheels of the Juggernaut of capital.[10]

Beginning with the dynamics of the economic system, Marx developed propositions that lead finally to a prediction of psychological consequence for individuals. The statement concerning estrangement from the intellectual potentialities of labor, together with other similar statements, is one basis for current formulations about alienation, a psychological condition that is one of the subjects of recent psychiatric discussion.

For the purposes of this discussion, the failures of Marxian theory are not as important as the general form it takes. The rise of effective industrial unions vitiated Marx's analysis near its premise, the irreversibility of the

9. K. Marx, *Capital* (New York: Modern Library, 1906), pp. 708-709.
10. *Ibid.*, p. 708.

law of capital accumulation. The form of his theory, however, provides an example of a social systemic model that does not include any aspects of individual systems of behavior. The question raised by this comparison is this: can we formulate a theory which somehow integrates both the individual and social systems of behavior?

Recently a number of writers have begun to develop an approach that gives more emphasis to social processes than does traditional psychiatric theory, yet does not neglect entirely individual aspects. Lemert, Erikson, and Goffman, among sociologists, and Szasz and Laing and Esterson, among psychiatrists, have contributed notably to this approach.[11] Lemert, particularly, by rejecting the more conventional concern with the origins of mental symptoms and stressing instead the potential importance of the societal reaction in stabilizing rule-breaking, focuses primarily on mechanisms of social control. The work of all these authors suggests research avenues that are analytically separable from questions of individual systems and point, therefore, to a theory that would incorporate social processes.

In his discussion of gamesmanship, Berne offers an analysis of alcoholism that is based on a social system model, rather than on an individual system model of alcoholism:

> In game analysis there is no such thing as alcoholism or "an alcoholic," but there is a role called the Alcoholic in a certain type of game. If a biochemical or physiological abnormality is the prime mover in excessive drinking—and that is still open to some question

11. E. M. Lemert, *Social Pathology* (New York: McGraw-Hill, 1951); K. T. Erikson, "Patient Role and Social Uncertainty—A Dilemma of the Mentally Ill," *Psychiatry*, 20 (August, 1957), pp. 263-274; E. Goffman, *Asylums* (New York: Doubleday-Anchor, 1961); T. S. Szasz, *The Myth of Mental Illness* (New York: Hoeber-Harper, 1961); R. D. Laing and A. Esterson, *Sanity, Madness and the Family*, (London: Tavistock Publications, 1964).

—then its study belongs in the field of internal medicine. Game analysis is interested in something quite different—the kinds of social transactions that are related to such excesses. Hence the game "Alcoholic."

In its full flower this is a five-handed game, although the roles may be condensed so that it starts off and terminates as a two-handed one. The central role is that of the Alcoholic—the one who is "it"—played by White. The chief supporting role is that of Persecutor, typically played by a member of the opposite sex, usually the spouse. The third role is that of Rescuer, usually played by someone of the same sex, often the good family doctor who is interested in the patient and also in drinking problems. In the classical situation the doctor successfully rescues the alcoholic from his habit. After White has not taken a drink for six months they congratulate each other. The following day White is found in the gutter.

The fourth role is that of the Patsy, or Dummy. In literature this is played by the delicatessen man who extends credit to White, gives him a sandwich on the cuff and perhaps a cup of coffee, without either persecuting him or trying to rescue him. In life this is more frequently played by White's mother, who gives him money and often sympathizes with him about the wife who does not understand him. In this aspect of the game, White is required to account in some plausible way for his need for money—by some project in which both pretend to believe, although they know what he is really going to spend most of the money for. Sometimes the Patsy slides over into another role, which is a helpful but not essential one: the Agitator, the "good guy" who offers supplies without even being asked for them: "Come have a drink with me (and you will go downhill faster)."

The ancillary professional in all drinking games is the bartender or liquor clerk. In the game "Alcoholic" he plays the fifth role, the Connection, the direct source of supply who also understands alcoholic talk, and who in a way is the most meaningful person in the life of any addict. The difference between the Connection and the other players is the difference between professionals and amateurs in any game: the professional knows when to stop. At a certain point a good bartender refuses to serve the Alcoholic, who is then left without any supplies unless he can locate a more indulgent Connection.[12]

Berne seems to be suggesting that the dynamics of alcoholism have less to do with the motivations and traits of the alcoholic than with the interactions between the occupants of the five interpersonal positions that he describes. According to his analysis, alcohol behavior is understandable only as an integral part of an interpersonal system.

A critique of the use of the medical model in psychiatry that parallels many aspects of the present discussion has been made by learning theorists in psychology. A thorough and well-documented statement can be found in the introduction to *Case Studies in Behavior Modification*.[13] The psychological model that is proposed as an alternative to the medical model is based on the stimulus-response arc. The resultant processes of diagnosis and treatment have been described simply by Eysenck:

Learning theory does not postulate any such "unconscious cause," but regards neurotic symptoms as simple learned habits; there is no neurosis underlying the symptom, but merely the symptom itself. *Get rid of the symptom and you have eliminated the neurosis*.[14]

The approach to mental disorder proposed by these researchers appears to be superior to the medical model

12. E. Berne, *Games People Play* (New York: Grove Press, 1964), pp. 73-74.
13. L. P. Ullmann and L. Krasner, *Case Studies in Behavior Modification* (New York: Holt, Rinehart and Winston, 1965).
14. H. J. Eysenck, "Learning Theory and Behavior Therapy," *Journal of Mental Science*, 105 (1959), pp. 61-75, quoted in Ullmann and Krasner, *op. cit.*, p. 2.

in three ways: first, it is behavioral, and therefore allows
for empirical research. Second, it is related to a systematic and explicitly stated body of propositions, i.e., learning theory. Finally, it is supported by a sizeable body of
empirical studies. It seems clear that this approach has
made important contributions to psychiatric theory and
practice, and is likely to lead to fruitful work in the
future.

At the same time, it should also be noted that "behavior modification," in practice, tends to be used as an
individual system model of mental disorder. Conceptually, this is not necessarily the case. Ullmann and Krasner conceptualize psychiatric symptoms as maladaptive
behavior. They go on to say that the goal of treatment
of maladaptive behavior should be to change the patient's relationship to environmental stimuli. This formulation does not prejudge the question of whether the
relationship should be changed by changing the patient
or the environment. But in listing the techniques used
in behavior modification, it is clear that the target for
these techniques is the patient. Such techniques as
"assertive responses, sexual responses, relaxation responses, conditioned avoidance responses, feeding responses, chemotherapy, expressive therapy, emotive
imagery, *in vivo* presentation of disruptive stimuli, model-
ing, negative practice, self-disclosure, extinction, selective positive reinforcement, and stimulus deprivation and
satiation" are the major techniques listed by Ullmann and
Krasner. These techniques are oriented toward changing
the patient's psychological system rather than the interpersonal or social system of which he is a member.
Furthermore, it is not clear how it is possible for the
therapist to effect changes through conditioning when
in actual fact the technique utilized by the therapist con-

stitute only a small fraction of the total environmental stimulation to which the patient is exposed.

Like the medical model, "behavior modification" tends to isolate the symptom from the context in which it occurs. This occurs even in carefully formulated statements such as that of Ullmann and Krasner. In their statement, they are very careful to relate maladaptive behavior to the social context:

Maladaptive behaviors are learned behaviors, and the development and maintenance of a maladaptive behavior is no different from the development and maintenance of any other behavior. There is no discontinuity between desirable and undesirable modes of adjustment or between "healthy" or "sick" behavior. The first major implication of this view is the question of how a behavior is to be identified as desirable or undesirable, adaptive or maladaptive. The general answer we propose is that because there are no disease entities involved in the majority of subjects displaying maladaptive behavior, the designation of a behavior as pathological or not is dependent upon the individual's society.[15]

To this point their formulation concerning "maladaptive behavior" exactly parallels the definition of deviant behavior presented here. They go on to further specify the meaning of maladaptive behavior in terms of roles and role reinforcement.

Specifically, while there are no single behaviors that would be said to be adaptive in all cultures, there are in all cultures definite expectations or roles for functioning adults in terms of familial and social responsibility. Along with role enactments, there are a full range of expected potential reinforcements. The person whose behavior is maladaptive does not fully live up to the expectations for one in his role, does not respond to all the stimuli actually

15. *Ibid.*, p. 20.

present, and does not obtain typical or maximum forms of reinforcement available to one of his status. . . . Maladaptive behavior is behavior that is considered inappropriate by those key people in a person's life who control reinforcers.[16]

Restated in sociological terms, their formulation is that deviance is the violation of social norms, and leads to negative social sanctions. Again, the parallel between the psychological and the sociological formulation is quite close.

This formulation of maladaptive behavior in terms of role expectations and reinforcement is potentially a powerful psychological tool, since it tends to bring in the mechanisms of social control, and provides a strong link, therefore, between individual and social system models of behavior. To maintain this link, however, it is necessary to remember that the classification of behavior as maladaptive is made relative to the standards of some particular society, and is not an absolute judgment. (The same reasoning is applicable, of course, to the concept of deviance.)

It appears to be very difficult to maintain a relativistic stance when the individual system models are used, particularly when the framework is transmitted to students. An instance of this difficulty is represented by the work of Sullivan and his students. Although Sullivan sought to take psychiatric symptoms out of the patient by defining them as disorders of interpersonal relationships, his students put them back in by defining mental illness as a deficiency in the *capacity* for interpersonal relations. This individualization of social system concepts can be seen in the Ullmann and Krasner formulation, when they define one criterion of maladaptive behavior as not responding to "all the stimuli actually present." Since the

16. *Idem.*

response to stimuli of anyone in any role is highly selective, it would seem that the definition at this point had reverted to the absolute definition of deviance in terms of individual pathology. One function of a social system model of mental disorder is to provide a framework for research which facilitates an approach to mental disorder which is free of the questionable assumptions of inherent pathology in psychiatric symptoms.

Of the formulations of anthropologists, the one which most nearly parallels the model described here is the biocultural model of Anthony F. C. Wallace.[17] Giving somewhat more emphasis to organic sources of rule-breaking, Wallace posits that the initial cause of mental illness is physiological, but that the cultural "mazeways" (cognitive maps) profoundly shape the course of illness. In some detail, he notes how the "theories" of illness of the sick individual, his family and associates, and the "professionals" impinge on illness as a behavior system. The chief components of a "theory" of illness are to be:

1. The specific *states* (normalcy, upset, psychosis, in treatment, and innovative personality).

2. The *transfer mechanisms* which explain (to the satisfaction of the member of the society) how the sick person moves from one state to another.

3. The *program* of illness and recovery which is described by the whole system.

Wallace gives an extended analysis of one particular syndrome, the Eskimo *pibloktoq*, an acute excitement sometimes known as Arctic hysteria. According to his theory, pibloktoq has a physiological base in calcium deficiency (hypocalcemia) but is shaped by the culture-

17. A. F. C. Wallace, "Mental Illness, Biology and Culture," in F. L. K. Hsu, *Psychological Anthropology* (Homewood, Ill.: The Dorsey Press, 1961), pp. 255-295.

bound interpretations made by the sick persons and those who deal with him. Following Wallace's model, Fogelson presents a detailed analysis of *windigo*, a syndrome of compulsive cannibalism reported among Northern Algonkian-speaking Indians, which emphasizes culture-bound interpretations of rule-breaking behavior.[18] The relationship between Wallace's model and the model developed here will be discussed later (Chapter 6, pp. 192-3).

The purpose of the present discussion is to state a set of nine propositions which make up basic assumptions for a social system model of mental disorder. This set is largely derived from the work of the authors listed above, all but two of the propositions (Nos. 4 and 5) being suggested, with varying degrees of explicitness, in the cited references. By stating these propositions explicitly, this theory attempts to facilitate testing of basic assumptions, all of which are empirically unverified, or only partly verified. By stating these assumptions in terms of standard sociological concepts, I attempt to show the relevance to studies of mental disorder of findings from diverse areas of social science, such as race relations and prestige suggestion. This theory also delineates three problems which are crucial for a sociological theory of mental disorder: what are the conditions in a culture under which diverse kinds of rule-breaking become stable and uniform; to what extent, in different phases of careers of mental patients, are symptoms of mental illness the result of conforming behavior; is there a general set of contingencies which lead to the definition of deviant behavior as a manifestation of mental illness? Finally, this discussion attempts to formulate special

18. R. D. Fogelson, "Psychological Theories of Windigo 'Psychosis' and a Preliminary Application of a Models Approach," in M. E. Spiro (ed.) *Context and Meaning in Cultural Anthropology* (New York: Free Press, 1965), pp. 74-99.

conceptual tools which are directly linked to sociological theory to deal with these problems. The social institution of insanity, residual rule-breaking, deviance, the social role of the mentally ill, and the bifurcation of the societal reaction into the alternative reactions of denial and labeling, are examples of such conceptual tools.

These conceptual tools are utilized to construct a theory of mental disorder in which psychiatric symptoms are considered to be labeled violations of social norms, and stable "mental illness" to be a social role. The validity of this theory depends upon verification of the nine propositions listed below in future studies, and should, therefore, be applied with caution, and with appreciation for its limitations. One such limitation is that the theory attempts to account for a much narrower class of phenomena than is usually found under the rubric of mental disorder; the discussion that follows will be focused exclusively on stable or recurring mental disorder, and does not explain the causes of single episodes. A second major limitation is that the theory probably distorts the phenomena under discussion. Just as the individual system models under-stress social processes, the model presented here probably exaggerates their importance. The social system model "holds constant" individual differences, in order to articulate the relationship between society and mental disorder. Ultimately, a framework which encompassed both individual and social systems, and distorted the contribution of neither, would be desirable. Given the present state of formulations in this area, this framework may prove useful by providing an explicit contrast to the more conventional medical and psychological approaches, and thus assisting in the formulation of socially oriented studies of mental disorder.

It should be made clear at this point that the purpose of this theory is *not* to reject psychiatric and psychological formulations in their totality. It is obvious that such formulations have served, and will continue to serve, useful functions in theory and practice concerning mental illness. The author's purpose, rather, is to develop a model which will complement the individual system models by providing a complete and explicit contrast. Although the individual system models of mental disorder have led to gains in research and treatment, they have also systematically obscured some aspects of the problem. The social system model, like the psychological model, highlights some aspects of the problem, and obscures others. It does, however, allow a fresh look at the field, since the problems it clarifies are apt to be those that are most obscure when viewed from the psychiatric or medical point of view

The case for the use of limited analytic models was clearly stated by Max Weber, for analysis which he called "one-sided":

The justification of the one-sided analysis of cultural reality from specific "points of view" . . . emerges purely as a technical expedient from the fact that training in the observation of the effects of qualitatively similar categories of causes and the repeated utilization of the same scheme of concepts and hypotheses offers all the advantages of the division of labor. It is free of the charge of arbitrariness to the extent that it is successful in producing insights into inter-connections which have been shown to be valuable in the causal explanation of concrete historical events.[19]

It can be argued that in addition to the advantages of the division of scientific labor, as suggested by Weber, there is yet another advantage to one-sided analysis. In

19. M. Weber, *The Methodology of the Social Sciences* (New York: Free Press, 1949), p. 71, quoted by D. Mechanic in H. J. Leavitt (ed.), *The Social Science of Organizations* (Englewood Cliffs, N.J.: Prentice-Hall, 1963), p. 167, in his discussion, "One-Sided Analysis Versus the Eclectic Approach."

the nature of scientific investigation, a central goal is the development of the "crucial experiment," a study whose results allow for the decisive comparison of two opposing theories, such that one is upheld and the other rejected. Implicit in the goal of the crucial experiment is the conception of science as an adversarial process, in which scientific progress arises out of the confrontation of explicitly conflicting theories. In his formulation of the history of change in the natural sciences, Kuhn considers all scientific progress as the conflict between "competing paradigms," i.e., opposing theories.[20] Whitehead has stated this view very clearly:

A clash of doctrines is not a disaster—it is an opportunity. . . . In formal logic, a contradiction is the signal of a defeat; but in the evolution of real knowledge it marks the first step in progress towards a victory.[21]

One road of progress in science is the intentional formulation of mutually incompatible models, each incomplete, and each explicating only a portion of the area under investigation. The advance of science, as in the theory of adversarial procedures in law, rests on the dialectical process which occurs when incommensurate positions are placed in conflict. In the present discussion of mental illness, the social system model is proposed not as an end in itself, but as the antithesis to the individual system model. By allowing for explicit consideration of these antithetical models, the way may be cleared for a synthesis, a model which has the advantages of both the individual and the social system models, but the disadvantages of neither.

20. T. Kuhn, *The Structure of Scientific Revolutions* (Chicago: University of Chicago Press, 1962).

21. A. N. Whitehead, *Science and the Modern World* (New York: Macmillan, 1962), pp. 266-267.

In the discussion that follows, a sociological theory of mental illness will first be developed. The theory, in turn, provides the framework for the field studies which are reported in the later part of the book. The theory has two basic components: social role and the societal reaction. Its key assumptions are that most chronic mental illness is at least in part a social role, and that the societal reaction is usually the most important determinant of entry into that role. Throughout the discussion that follows, this sociological model will continually be compared with and contrasted with the more conventional medical and psychological models of mental illness, in an attempt to delineate significant problems for further analysis and research.

Part I of the book, in addition to this introduction, has two further chapters, each of which is concerned with the statement of the theory of mental illness. Chapter 2 is devoted to the basic premise of the theory: symptoms of mental illness are violations of residual rules. In this analysis, "mental illness" is considered, therefore, as residual deviance. Discussion of propositions concerning the origins, prevalence, and duration and consequences of residual deviance are found in this chapter.

In Chapter 3, "The Social Institution of Insanity," the rest of the theory is outlined. The first two sections of the chapter concern the social role of the mentally ill: how and why the role is played, and the source of the role-imagery in ordinary language and in the mass media. The last two sections of the chapter deal with the social system and its relation to deviant careers. This section contains a discussion of the part played by the societal reaction to rule-breaking in causing or blocking entry into the role and status of the mentally ill. The final section describes the entire theory as a model, in which the rule-breaking acts, the responses of others, and the rule-breaker's responses to these responses, and so on, are seen as constituting a system with definite boundaries and self-maintaining properties. The discussion of the social system model completes Part I.

Part II describes several studies that I conducted, which were based on the theory outlined in Part I and which provide, in turn, support for certain aspects of the theory. In Chapter 4, the problem of uncertainty in diagnosis, and the physician's reaction to uncertainty is explored. It is suggested that physicians tend to follow the rule, "when in doubt, diagnose illness, rather than health." Some of the implications and consequences of this rule are then discussed.

In the next chapter, two field studies are reported that show how crucial the problem of the physician's response to uncertainty becomes in the handling of mental patients. The first study in Chapter 5 concerns the decision to hospitalize and treat; the second study, the decision to release. Both studies provide very strong support for one of the central theses of the book: at the present time, the variables that afford the best understanding and prediction of the course of "mental illness" are not the refined etiological and nosological features of the illness, but gross features of the community and legal and psychiatric procedures. (See Proposition 9, and the discussion that follows it, in Chapter 3)

The final chapter explores some of the implications of the theory and research in the earlier chapters. The first section deals with the way in which behavior may or may not be seen as a psychiatric symptom, depending on the social context in which it occurs, and the preconceptions and procedures used by the diagnostician. Following from this discussion, a research proposal is outlined for making the diagnostic practices of health, custodial, and welfare organizations a subject for systematic research. The next section presents a description of the course of mental illness in terms of the structure and dynamics of social status: the distinction between sanity and insanity is depicted as a status system with many similarities to the "color line." This analysis raises a number of questions concerning theory and research, and public policy.

The final section of Chapter 6 summarizes the argument and concludes the book. In the Appendix, a short explanation of the development and significance of the flow chart in Chapter 3 is provided by Walter Buckley. Having outlined the contents of the book, we are now ready for Chapter 2, on residual deviance.

2

ONE source of immediate embarrassment to any social theory of "mental illness" is that the terms used in referring to these phenomena in our society prejudge the issue. The medical metaphor "mental illness" suggests a determinate process which occurs within the individual: the unfolding and development of disease. In order to avoid this assumption, we will utilize sociological, rather than medical concepts to formulate the problem. Particularly crucial to the formulation of the problem is the idea of psychiatric "symptoms," which is applied to the behavior that is taken to signify the existence of an underlying mental illness. Since in the great majority of cases of mental illness, the existence of this underlying illness is unproven, we need to discuss "symptomatic" behavior in terms that do not involve the assumption of illness.

Two concepts seem to be suited best to the task of discussing psychiatric symptoms from a sociological point of view: rule-breaking and deviance. Rule-breaking refers to behavior which is in clear violation of the agreed-upon rules of the group. These rules are usually discussed by sociologists as social norms. If the symptoms of mental illness are to be construed as violations of social norms, it is necessary to specify the type of norms involved. Most norm violations do not cause the violator to be labeled as mentally ill, but as ill-mannered, ignorant, sinful, criminal, or perhaps just harried, depending on the type of norm involved. There are innumerable norms, however, over which consensus is so complete that the members of a group appear to take them for granted. A host of such norms surround even the simplest conversation: a person engaged in conversation is expected to face toward his partner, rather than directly away from him; if his gaze is toward the partner he is expected to look toward the other's eyes, rather than, say, toward his forehead; to stand at a proper conversational distance, neither one inch away nor across the room, and so on. A person who regularly violated these expectations probably would not be thought to be merely ill-bred, but as strange, bizarre, and frightening, because his behavior violates the assumptive world of the group, the world that is construed to be the only one that is natural, decent, and possible.

The concept of deviance used here will follow Becker's usage. He argues that deviance can be most usefully considered as a quality of people's response to an act, rather than as a characteristic of the act itself.

Social groups create deviance by making the rules whose infraction constitutes deviance, and by applying those rules to *particular people* and labeling them as outsiders . . . deviance is not a quality of the act the person commits, but rather a consequence of the application by others of rules and sanctions to an "offender." *The deviant is one to whom that label has successfully been applied;* deviant behavior is behavior that people so label.[1] [Italics rearranged.]

By this definition, deviants are not a group of people who have committed the same act, but are a group of people who have been stigmatized as deviants.

1. H. S. Becker, *Outsiders* (New York: Free Press, 1963), p. 9.

Becker argues that the distinction between rule-breaking and deviance is necessary for scientific purposes:

Since deviance is, among other things, a consequence of the responses of others to a person's act, students of deviance cannot assume that they are dealing with a homogeneous category when they study people who have been labeled deviant. That is, they cannot assume that these people have actually . . . broken some rule, because the process of labeling may not be infallible. . . . Furthermore, they cannot assume that the category of those labeled deviant will contain all those who actually have broken a rule, for many offenders may escape apprehension and thus fail to be included in the population of "deviants" they study. Insofar as the category lacks homogeneity and fails to include all the cases that belong in it, one cannot reasonably expect to find common factors of personality or life situation that will account for the supposed deviance.[2]

For the purpose of this discussion, we will conform to Becker's separation of rule-breaking and deviance. Rule-breaking will refer to a class of acts, violations of social norms, and deviance to particular acts which have been publicly and officially labeled as norm violations.

Using Becker's distinction, we can categorize most psychiatric symptoms as instances of residual rule-breaking or residual deviance. The culture of the group provides a vocabulary of terms for categorizing many norm violations: crime, perversion, drunkenness, and bad manners are familiar examples. Each of these terms is derived from the type of norm broken, and ultimately, from the type of behavior involved. After exhausting these categories, however, there is always a residue of the most diverse kinds of violations, for which the culture provides

2. *Idem.*

no explicit label. For example, although there is great cultural variation in what is defined as decent or real, each culture tends to reify its definition of decency and reality, and so provides no way of handling violations of its expectations in these areas. The typical norm governing decency or reality, therefore, literally "goes without saying" and its violation is unthinkable for most of its members. For the convenience of the society in construing those instances of unnamable rule-breaking which are called to its attention, these violations may be lumped together into a residual category: witchcraft, spirit possession, or, in our own society, mental illness. In this discussion, the diverse kinds of rule-breaking for which our society provides no explicit label, and which, therefore, sometimes lead to the labeling of the violator as mentally ill, will be considered to be technically *residual rule-breaking*.

Let us consider further some of the implications of a definition of psychiatric "symptoms" as instances of residual deviance. In *Behavior in Public Places*, Goffman develops the idea that there is a complex of social norms that regulate the way in which a person may behave when he is in the presence, or potentially in the presence, of other persons.[3] Goffman's discussion of the norms regarding "involvement," particularly, illustrates how such psychiatric symptoms as withdrawal and hallucinations may be regarded as violations of residual rules.

Noting that lolling and loitering are usually specifically prohibited in codes of law, Goffman goes on to point out that there is a much more elaborate set of norms centering around the expectation that a person appearing in public should be involved or engaged in doing something:

3. E. Goffman, *Behavior in Public Places* (New York: Free Press, 1964).

The rule against "having no purpose," or being disengaged, is evident in the exploitation of untaxing involvements to rationalize or mask desired lolling—a way of covering one's physical presence in a situation with a veneer of acceptable visible activity. Thus when individuals want a "break" in their work routine, they may remove themselves to a place where it is acceptable to smoke and there smoke in a pointed fashion. Certain minimal "recreational" activities are also used as covers for disengagement, as in the case of "fishing" off river banks where it is guaranteed that no fish will disturb one's reverie, or "getting a tan" on the beach—activity that shields reverie or sleep, although, as with hoboes' lolling, a special uniform may have to be worn, which proclaims and institutionalizes the relative inactivity. As might be expected, when the context firmly provides a dominant involvement that is outside the situation, as when riding in a train or airplane, then gazing out the window, or reverie, or sleeping may be quite permissible. In short, the more the setting guarantees that the participant has not withdrawn from what he ought to be involved in, the more liberty it seems he will have to manifest what would otherwise be considered withdrawal in the situation.[4]

The rule requiring that an adult be "involved" when in public view is unstated in our society, yet so taken for granted that individuals almost automatically shield their lack of involvement in socially acceptable ways, as illustrated in the quotation. Thus the rule of involvement would seem to be a residual rule.

Two types of involvements that Goffman discusses are particularly relevant to a discussion of residual deviance: "away," and "occult involvements." "Away" is described in this manner:

While outwardly participating in an activity within a social situation, an individual can allow his attention to turn from what he and

4. *Ibid.*, pp. 58-59.

everyone else considered the real or serious world, and give himself
up for a time to a playlike world in which he alone participates.
This kind of inward emigration from the gathering may be called
"away," and we find that strict regulations obtain regarding it.

Perhaps the most important kind of away is that through
which the individual relives some past experiences or rehearses
some future ones, this taking the form of what is variously called
reverie, brown study, woolgathering, daydreaming or autistic thinking. At such times the individual may demonstrate his absence
from the current situation by a preoccupied, faraway look in his
eyes, or by a sleeplike stillness of his limbs, or by that special
class of side involvements that can be sustained in an utterly "unconscious" abstracted manner—humming, doodling, drumming the
fingers on a table, hair twisting, nose picking, scratching.[5]

This discussion is relevant to the psychiatric symptoms
which come under the rubric of "withdrawal," showing
that the behavior which is called withdrawal in itself
is not socially unacceptable. An "away" is met with public censure only when it occurs in a socially unacceptable
context. But this is to say that there are residual rules
governing the context in which aways may take place.
When an away violates these rules, it is apt to be called
withdrawal, and taken as evidence of mental illness.

"Occult involvement" is defined as a subtype of
awayness:

. . . There is a kind of awayness where the individual gives others
the impression, whether warranted or not, that he is not aware that
he is "away." This is the area of what psychiatry terms "hallucinations" and delusionary states. Corresponding to these "unnatural"
verbal activities, there are unnatural bodily ones, where the individual's .activity is patiently tasklike but not "understandable"
or "meaningful." The unnatural action may even involve the hold-

5. *Ibid.*, pp. 69-70.

ing or grasping of something, as when an adult mental patient retains a tight hold on a doll or a fetish-like piece of cloth. Here the terms "mannerism," "ritual act," or "posturing" are applied, which, like the term "unnatural," are clear enough in their way but hardly tell us with any specificity what it is that characterizes "natural" acts.[6]

At first glance it would seem that if there was ever a type of behavior that in itself would be seen as abnormal, it would be occult involvements. As Goffman notes, however, there is an element of cultural definition even with occult involvements:

There are societies in which conversation with a spirit not present is as acceptable when sustained by properly authorized persons as is conversation over a telephone in American society.[7]

Furthermore, he points out that even in American society, there are occasions in which occult involvement is not censured:

Those who attend a seance would not consider it inappropriate for the medium to interact with "someone on the other side," whether they believe this to be staged or a genuine interaction. And certainly we define praying as acceptable when done at proper occasions.[8]

Thus talking to spirits or praying to God are not improper in themselves; indeed they are seen as legitimate modes of activity when they follow the proprieties—i.e., when they occur in the socially proper circumstances, and are conducted by persons recognized as legitimately, even though occultly, involved.

Two significant implications follow from this discus-

6. *Ibid.*, pp. 75-76.
7. *Ibid.*, p. 79.
8. *Idem.*

sion of the etiquette of involvement. The first is that such psychiatric symptoms as withdrawal, hallucinations, continual muttering, posturing, etc., may be categorized as violations of certain social norms—those norms which are so taken for granted that they are not explicitly verbalized, which we have called residual rules. In particular instances discussed here, the residual rule concerned involvement in public places. It is true, of course, that various specific aspects of the involvement rule occasionally are found, for example, in books of etiquette. Here for example, is a typical proscription concerning involvement with one's own person in public places:

Men should never look in the mirror nor comb their hair in public. At most a man may straighten his necktie and smooth his hair with his hand. It is probably unnecessary to add that it is most unattractive to scratch one's head, to rub one's face or touch one's teeth, or to clean one's fingernails in public. All these things should be done privately.[9]

Although many such informal rules could be pointed to, it is important to note that they are all situationally specific. There is nowhere codified a general principle of involvement, or even self-involvement. Unlike codified principles, such as the Ten Commandments, it is one of those expectations which it is felt should govern the behavior of every decent person, even though it goes unsaid. Because it goes unsaid, we are not equipped by our culture to smoothly categorize violations of such a rule, but rather may resort to a residual catch-all category of violations, i.e., symptoms of mental illness.

If it proves to be correct that most symptoms of mental illness can be systematically classified as violations of culturally particular normative networks, then

9. M. Fenwick, *Vogue's Book of Etiquette* (New York: Simon and Schuster, 1948), p. 11, quoted in Goffman, *op. cit.*

these symptoms may be removed from the realm of universal physical events, where they now tend to be placed by psychiatric theory, along with other culture-free symptoms such as fever, and be investigated sociologically and anthropologically, like any other item of social behavior.

A second implication of the redefinition of psychiatric symptoms as residual deviance is the great emphasis that this perspective puts on the context in which the "symptomatic" behavior occurs. As Goffman repeatedly shows, "aways," occult involvements, and other kinds of rule violations do not in themselves bring forth censure; it is only when socially unqualified persons perform these acts, or perform them in inappropriate contexts. That is, these acts are objectionable when they occur in a manner that does not conform to the unstated, but nevertheless operative, etiquette that governs them. Although recently psychiatric discussions of symptomatology have begun to display considerable interest in the social context, it is still true that psychiatric diagnosis tends to focus on the pattern of symptomatic behavior itself, to the neglect of the context in which the symptom occurs. The significance of this tendency in psychiatric diagnostic procedures will be discussed later.[10] The remainder of this chapter will be devoted to a discussion of the origins, prevalence, and course of the behavior that we have defined here as residual rule-breaking.

THE ORIGINS OF RESIDUAL RULE-BREAKING

It is customary in psychiatric research to seek a single generic source or at best a small number of sources for

---

10. See Chapter 5, on the relationship between symptoms, context, and meaning.

mental illness. The redefinition of psychiatric symptoms
as residual deviance immediately suggests, however, that
there should be an unlimited number of sources of deviance. The first proposition is therefore:

1. *Residual rule-breaking arises from fundamentally
diverse sources.* Four distinct types of sources will be
discussed here: organic, psychological, external stress, and
volitional acts of innovation or defiance. The organic and
psychological origins of residual rule-breaking are widely
noted and will not be discussed at length here. It has
been demonstrated repeatedly that particular cases of
mental disorder had their origin in genetic, bio-chemical
or physiological conditions. Psychological sources are
also frequently indicated: peculiarity of up-bringing and
training have been reported often, particularly in the
psychoanalytic literature. The great majority of precise
and systematic studies of causation of mental disorder
have been limited to either organic or psychological
sources.

It is widely granted, however, that psychiatric symptoms can also arise from external stress: from drug ingestion, the sustained fear and hardship of combat, and
from deprivation of food, sleep, and even sensory experience. Excerpts from reports on the consequences of
stress will illustrate the rule-breaking behavior that is
generated by this less familiar source.

Physicians have long known that toxic substances can
cause psychotic-like symptoms, when ingested in appropriate doses. Recently a wide variety of substances have
been the subject of experimentation in producing "model
psychoses." Drugs such as mescaline and LSD-25, particularly, have been described as producing fairly close
replicas of psychiatric symptoms, such as visual hallucina-

tions, loss of orientation to space and time, interference with thought processes, etc. Here is an excerpt from a report by a person who had taken LSD–25, who was a qualified psychologist:

One concomitant of LSD that I shared with other subjects was distortion of the time sense. The subjective clock appeared to race. This was observed even at 25 milligrams in counting 60 seconds. My tapping rate was also speeded up. On the larger dose (½ gram) my time sense was dipslaced by hours. I thought the afternoon was well spent when it was only 1:00 P.M. I could look at my watch and realize the error, but I continued to be disoriented in time. The time sense depends on the way time is "filled," and I was probably responding to the quickened tempo of experience.

This was in fact, my overwhelming impression of LSD. Beginning with the physiological sensations (lightheadedness, excitement) I was shortly flooded by a montage of ideas, images, and feelings that seemed to thrust themselves upon me unbidden. I had glimpses of very bright thoughts, like a fleeting insight into the psychotic process, which I wanted to write down. . . . But they pushed each other aside. Once gone, they could not be recaptured because the parade of new images could not be stopped.[11]

The time disorientation described is a familiar psychiatric symptom, as is the ideational "pressure," which is usually described as a feature of manic excitement.

Combat psychosis and psychiatric symptoms arising from starvation have been repeatedly described in the psychiatric literature. Psychotic symptoms resulting from sleeplessness are less familiar. One instance will be used to illustrate this reaction. Brauchi and West reported the symptoms of two participants in a radio marathon, which

11. C. C. Bennett, "The Drugs and I," in L. Uhr and J. G. Miller (eds.), *Drugs and Behavior* (New York: Wiley, 1960), pp. 606-607.

required them to talk alternately every thirty minutes.[12] After 168 hours, one of the contestants felt that he and his opponent belonged to a secret club of nonsleepers. He accused his girl-friend of kissing an observer, even though she was with him at the time. He felt he was being punished, had transient auditory and visual hallucinations and became suggestible, he and his opponent exhibiting a period of *folie à deux* when the delusions and hallucinations of the one were accepted by the other. He showed persistence of his psychotic symptoms, with delusions about secret agents, and felt that he was responsible for the Israeli-Egyptian conflict. His reactions contain many elements which psychiatrists would describe as paranoid and depressive features.

There have been a number of recent studies which show that deprivation of sensory stimulation can cause hallucinations and other symptoms. In one such study Heron reported on subjects who were cut off from sensations:

Male college students were paid to lie 24 hours a day on a comfortable bed in a lighted semi-soundproof cubicle . . . wearing translucent goggles which admitted diffuse light but prevented pattern vision. Except when eating or at toilet, they wore cotton gloves and cardboard cuffs . . . in order to limit tactile perceptions.[13]

The subjects stayed from two to three days. Twenty-five of the 29 subjects reported hallucinations, which usually were initially simple, and became progressively more complex over time. Three of the subjects believed their visions to be real:

12. J. T. Brauchi and L. J. West, "Sleep Deprivation," *Journal of the American Medical Association*, 171 (1959), p. 11.
13. W. Heron, "Cognitive and Physiological Effects of Perceptual Isolation," in P. Solomon *et al.* (eds.), *Sensory Deprivation*, (Cambridge, Mass.: Harvard University Press, 1961), p. 8.

One man thought that he saw things coming at him and showed head withdrawal quite consistently when this happened; a second was convinced that we were projecting pictures on his goggles by some sort of movie camera; a third felt that someone else was in the cubicle with him.[14]

Merely monotonous environments, as in long-distance driving or flying, are now thought to be capable of generating symptoms. The following excerpt is taken from a series on psychiatric symptoms in military aviation:

A pilot was flying a bomber at 40,000 feet and had been continuing straight and level for about an hour. There was a haze over the ground which prevented a proper view and rendered the horizon indistinct. The other member of the crew was sitting in a separate place out of the pilot's view, and the two men did not talk to each other. Suddenly the pilot felt detached from his surroundings and then had the strong impression that the aircraft had one wing down and was turning. Without consulting his instruments he corrected the attitude, but the aircraft went to a spiral dive because it had in fact been flying straight and level. The pilot was very lucky to recover from the spiral dive, and when he landed the airframe was found to be distorted [from the stress caused by the dive].

On examining the pilot, no psychiatric abnormality was found. . . . As the man had no wish to give up flying and was in fact physically and mentally fit, he was offered an explanation of the phenomenon and was reassured. He returned to flying duties.[15]

In this case, the symptoms (depersonalization and spatial disorientation) occurring as they did in a real-life situation, could easily have resulted in a fatal accident. In laboratory studies of model psychoses, the consequences

14. *Ibid.*, p. 17.
15. A. M. H. Bennett, "Sensory Deprivation in Aviation," in Solomon, *op. cit.*, p. 166.

are usually easily controlled. Particularly relevant to this discussion is the role of reassurance of the subject by the experimenter, after the experiment is over.

In all of the laboratory studies (as in this last case as well), the persons who have had "psychotic" experiences are reassured; they are told, for example, that the experiences they had were solely due to the situation that they were placed in, and that anyone else placed in such a situation would experience similar sensations. In other words, the implications of the rule-breaking for the rule-breaker's social status and self-conception are *denied*. Suppose, however, for purposes of argument, that a diabolical experiment were performed in which subjects, after having exhibited the psychotic symptoms under stress, were "labeled." That is, they were told that the symptoms were not a normal reaction, but a reliable indication of deep-seated psychological disorder in their personality. Suppose, in fact, that such labeling were continued in their ordinary lives. Would such a labeling process stabilize rule-breaking which would have otherwise been transitory? This question will be considered under Proposition 3, following, and in Chapter 3.

Returning to the consideration of origins, rule-breaking finally can be seen as a volitional act of innovation or rebellion. Two examples from art history illustrate the deliberate breaking of residual rules. It is reported that the early reactions of the critics and the public to the paintings of the French impressionists was one of disbelief and dismay; the colors, particularly, were thought to be so unreal as to be evidence of madness. It is ironic that in the ensuing struggle, the Impressionists and their followers effected some changes in the color norms of the public. Today we accept the colors of the Impressionists (as in Pepsi-Cola ads) without a second glance.

The Dada movement provides an example of an art movement deliberately conceived to violate, and thereby reject, existing standards of taste and value. The jewel-encrusted book of Dada, which was to contain the greatest treasures of contemporary civilization, was found to be filled with toilet-paper, grass, and similar materials. A typical *objet d'art* produced by Dadaism was a fur-lined teacup. A climactic event in the movement was the Dada Exposition given at the Berlin Opera House. All of the celebrities of the German art world and dignitaries of the Weimar Republic were invited to attend the opening night. The first item of the evening was a poetry-reading contest, in which there were fourteen contestants. Since the fourteen read their poems simultaneously, the evening soon ended in a riot.

The examples of residual rule-breaking given here are not presented as scientifically impeccable instances of this type of behavior. There are many problems connected with reliability in these areas, particularly with the material on behavior resulting from drug ingestion, and sleep and sensory deprivation. Much of this material is simply clinical or autobiographical impressions of single, isolated instances. In the studies that have been conducted, insufficient attention is usually paid to research design, systematic techniques of data collection, and devices to guard against experimenter or subject bias.

Of the many questions of a more general nature that are posed by these examples, one of the more interesting is: are the "model psychoses" produced by drugs, or food, sleep, or sensory deprivation actually identical to "natural" psychoses, or, on the other hand, are the similarities only superficial, masking fundamental differences between the laboratory and the natural rule-breaking? The opinions of researchers are split on this issue. Many in-

vestigators state that model and real psychoses are basically the same. According to a recent report, in the
autobiographical, clinical, and experimental accounts of
sensory deprivation, Bleuler's cardinal symptoms of
schizophrenia frequently appear: disturbances of associations, disharmony of affect, autism, ambivalence, dis-
ruption of secondary thought processes accompanied by
regression to primary processes, impairment of reality-
testing capacity, distortion of body image, depersonalization, delusions, and hallucinations.[16] Other researchers,
however, insist that there are fundamental differences
between experimental and genuine psychoses.

The controversy over model psychoses provides evidence of a basic difficulty in the scientific study of mental
disorder. Although there is an enormous literature on the
description of psychiatric symptoms, at this writing, scientifically respectable descriptions of the major psychiatric symptoms, that is to say, descriptions which have
been shown to be precise, reliable, and valid, do not
exist.[17] It is not only that studies which demonstrate the
precision, reliability, and validity of measures of symptomatic behavior have not been made, but that the very
basis of such studies, operational definitions of psychiatric
symptoms, have yet to be formulated. In physical medicine, there are instruments that yield easily verified, re-
peatable measures of disease symptoms; the thermometer
used in detecting the presence of fever is an obvious
example. The analogous instruments in psychiatric medicine, questionnaires, behavior rating scales, etc., which
yield verifiable measures of the presence of some symp-

16. N. Rosenzweig, "Sensory Deprivation and Schizophrenia: Some
Clinical and Theoretical Similarities," *American Journal of Psychiatry*,
116 (1959), p. 326.
17. W. A. Scott, "Research Definitions of Mental Health and Mental
Illness," *Psychological Bulletin*, 55 (January, 1958), pp. 29-45.

tom pattern (paranoid ideation, for example) have yet
to be found, tested, and agreed upon.

In the absence of scientifically acceptable evidence,
we can only rely on our own assessment of the evidence,
in conjunction with our appraisal of the conflicting
opinions of the psychiatric investigators. In this case,
there is at present no conclusive answer, but the weight
of evidence seems to be that there is some likelihood that
the model psychoses are not basically dissimilar to ordinary psychoses. Therefore it appears that the first proposition, that there are many diverse sources of residual
rule-breaking, is supported by available knowledge.

PREVALENCE

The second proposition concerns the prevalence of
residual rule-breaking in entire and ostensibly normal
populations. This prevalence is roughly analogous to
what medical epidemiologists call the "total" or "true"
prevalence of mental symptoms.

2. *Relative to the rate of treated mental illness, the
rate of unrecorded residual rule-breaking is extremely
high.* There is evidence that gross violations of rules are
often not noticed or, if noticed, rationalized as eccentricity. Apparently, many persons who are extremely
withdrawn, or who "fly off the handle" for extended
periods of time, who imagine fantastic events, or who
hear voices or see visions, are not labeled as insane either
by themselves or others.[18] Their rule-breaking, rather, is

18. See, for example, J. A. Clausen and M. R. Yarrow, "Paths to
the Mental Hospital," *Journal of Social Issues*, 11 (December, 1955),
pp. 25-32; A. B. Hollingshead and F. C. Redlich, *Social Class and
Mental Illness* (New York: Wiley, 1958), pp. 172-176; and E. and J.
Cumming, *Closed Ranks* (Cambridge, Mass.: Harvard University Press,
1957), pp. 92-103.

unrecognized, ignored, or rationalized. This pattern of inattention and rationalization will be called "denial."[19]

In addition to the kind of evidence cited above there are a number of epidemiological studies of total prevalence. There are numerous problems in interpreting the results of these studies; the major difficulty is that the definition of mental disorder is different in each study, as are the methods used to screen cases. These studies represent, however, the best available information and can be used to estimate total prevalence.

A convenient summary of findings is presented in Plunkett and Gordon.[20] These authors compare the methods and populations used in eleven field studies, and list rates of total prevalence (in percentage) as 1.7, 3.6, 4.5, 4.7, 5.3, 6.1, 10.9, 13.8, 23.2, 23.3, and 33.3.

Since the Plunkett and Gordon review was published two elaborate studies of symptom prevalence have appeared, one in Manhattan, the other in Nova Scotia.[21] In the Midtown Manhattan study it is reported that 80 per cent of the sample currently had at least one psychiatric symptom. Probably more comparable to the earlier studies is their rating of "impaired because of psychiatric illness," which was applied to 23.4 per cent of the population. In the Stirling County studies, the estimate of current prevalence is 57 per cent, with 20 per cent classified as "Psychiatric Disorder with Significant Impairment."

How do these total rates compare with the rates of treated mental disorder? One of the studies cited by

19. The term "denial" is used in the same sense as in Cumming and Cumming, *ibid.*, Chapter VII.
20. R. J. Plunkett and J. E. Gordon, *Epidemiology and Mental Illness* (New York: Basic Books, 1960).
21. L. Srole *et al.*, *Mental Health in the Metropolis* (New York: McGraw-Hill, 1962); D. C. Leighton *et al.*, *The Character of Danger* (New York: Basic Books, 1963).

Plunkett and Gordon, the Baltimore study reported by Pasamanick, is useful in this regard since it includes both treated and untreated rates.[22] As compared with the untreated rate of 10.9 per cent, the rate of treatment in state, VA, and private hospitals of Baltimore residents was 0.5 per cent.[23] That is, for every mental patient there were approximately 20 untreated persons located by the survey. It is possible that the treated rate is too low, however, since patients treated by private physicians were not included. Judging from another study, the New Haven study of treated prevalence, the number of patients treated in private practice is small in comparison with those hospitalized: over 70 per cent of the patients located in that study were hospitalized even though extensive case-finding techniques were employed. The overall treated prevalence in the New Haven study was reported as 0.8 per cent, a figure that is in good agreement with my estimate of 0.7 per cent for the Baltimore study.[24] If we accept 0.8 per cent as an estimate of the upper limit of treated prevalence for the Pasamanick study, the ratio of treated to untreated patients is 1:14. That is, for every patient we should expect to find 14 untreated cases in the community.

One interpretation of this finding is that the untreated patients in the community represent those with less severe disorders, while patients with severe impairments all fall into the treated group. Some of the findings in the Pasamanick study point in this direction. Of the untreated patients, about half are classified as psychoneurotic. Of the psychoneurotics, in turn, about half again are classified as suffering from minimal impairment. At

22. B. Pasamanick, "A Survey of Mental Disease in an Urban Population: IV. An Approach to Total Prevalence Rates," *Archives of General Psychiatry*, 5 (August, 1961), pp. 151-155.

23. *Ibid.*, p. 153.

24. Hollingshead and Redlich, *op. cit.*, p. 199.

least a fourth of the untreated group, then, involved very mild disorders.[25]

The evidence from the group diagnosed as psychotic does not support this interpretation, however. Almost all of the persons diagnosed as psychotic were judged to have severe impairment; yet half of the diagnoses of psychosis occurred in the untreated group. In other words, according to this study, there were as many untreated as treated cases of psychoses.[26]

In the Manhattan study, a direct comparison by age group was made between the most deviant group (those classified as "incapacitated") and persons actually receiving psychiatric treatment. The results for the groups of younger age (twenty to forty years) is similar to that in the Pasamanick study: treated prevalence is roughly 0.6 per cent, and the proportion classified as "incapacitated" is about 1.5 per cent. In the older age group, however, the ratio of treated to treatable changes abruptly. The treated prevalence is about 0.5 per cent, but 4 per cent are designated as "incapacitated" in the population. In the older group, therefore, the ratio of treatable to treated[27] is about 8 : 1.

Once again, because of lack of complete comparability between studies, conflicting results, and inadequate research designs, the evidence regarding prevalence is not conclusive. The existing weight of evidence appears, however, very strongly to support Proposition 2.

THE DURATION AND CONSEQUENCES
OF RESIDUAL RULE-BREAKING

In most epidemiological research, it is frequently assumed that treated prevalence is an excellent index of

25. Pasamanick, *op. cit.*, pp. 153-154.
26. *Ibid.*
27. Srole, *loc. cit.*

total prevalence. The community studies discussed above, however, suggest that the majority of cases of "mental illness" never receive medical attention. This finding has great significance for a crucial question about residual deviance: given a typical instance of residual rule-breaking, what is its expected course and consequences? Or, to put the same question in medical language, what is the prognosis for a case in which psychiatric signs and symptoms are evident?

The usual working hypothesis for physicians confronted with a sign or symptom is that of progressive development as the inner logic of disease unfolds. The medical framework thus leads one to expect that unless medical intervention occurs, the signs and symptoms of disease are usually harbingers of further, and more serious, consequences for the individual showing the symptoms. This is not to say, of course, that physicians think of all symptoms as being parts of a progressive disease pattern; witness the concept of the "benign" condition. The point is that the imagery which the medical model calls up tends to predispose the physician toward expecting that symptoms are but initial signs of further illness.

The finding that the great majority of persons displaying psychiatric symptoms go untreated leads to the third proposition:

3. *Most residual rule-breaking is "denied" and is of transitory significance.* The enormously high rates of total prevalence suggest that most residual rule-breaking is unrecognized or rationalized away. For this type of rule-breaking, which is amorphous and uncrystallized, Lemert used the term "primary deviation."[28] Balint describes similar behavior as "the unorganized phase of

28. Lemert, *op. cit.*, Chapter 4.

illness."[29] Although Balint assumes that patients in this phase ultimately "settle down" to an "organized illness," other outcomes are possible. A person in this stage may "organize" his deviance in other than illness terms, e.g., as eccentricity or genius, or the rule-breaking may terminate when situational stress is removed.

The experience of battlefield psychiatrists can be interpreted to support the hypothesis that residual rule-breaking is usually transitory. Glass reports that combat neurosis is often self-terminating if the soldier is kept with his unit and given only the most superficial medical attention.[30] Descriptions of child behavior can be interpreted in the same way. According to these reports, most children go through periods in which at least several of the following kinds of rule-breaking may occur: temper tantrums, head banging, scratching, pinching, biting, fantasy playmates or pets, illusory physical complaints, and fears of sounds, shapes, colors, persons, animals, darkness, weather, ghosts, and so on.[31] In the vast majority of instances, however, these behavior patterns do not become stable.

There are, of course, conditions which do fit the model of a progressively unfolding disease. In the case of a patient exhibiting psychiatric symptoms because of general paresis, the early signs and symptoms appear to be good, though not perfect, indicators of later more serious deterioration of both physical health and social behavior. Conditions that have been demonstrated to be

29. M. Balint, *The Doctor, His Patient, and the Illness* (New York: International Universities Press, 1957), p. 18.

30. A. J. Glass, "Psychotherapy in the Combat Zone," in *Symposium on Stress* (Washington, D.C.: Army Medical Service Graduate School, 1953). *Cf.* A. Kardiner and H. Spiegel, *War Stress and Neurotic Illness* (New York: Hoeber, 1947), Chapters III-IV.

31. F. L. Ilg and L. B. Ames, *Child Behavior* (New York: Dell, 1960), pp. 138-188.

of this type are relatively rare, however. Paresis, which was once a major category of mental disease, accounts today for only a very minor proportion of mental patients under treatment. Proposition 3 would appear to fit the great majority of mental patients, in whom external stress such as family conflict, fatigue, drugs and similar factors are often encountered.

Of the first three propositions, the last is both the most crucial for the theory as a whole and the least well supported by existing evidence. It is not a matter of there being great amounts of negative evidence, showing that psychiatric symptoms are reliable indicators of subsequent disease, but that there is little evidence of any kind concerning development of symptoms over time. There are a number of analogies in the history of physical medicine, however, which are suggestive. For example, until the late 1940s, histoplasmosis was thought to be a rare tropical disease, with a uniformly fatal outcome.[32] Recently, however, it has been discovered that it is widely prevalent, and with fatal outcome or even impairment extremely unusual. It is conceivable that most "mental illnesses" may prove to follow the same pattern, when adequate longitudinal studies of cases in normal populations have been made.

If residual rule-breaking is highly prevalent among ostensibly "normal" persons and is usually transitory, as suggested by the last two propositions, what accounts for the small percentage of residual rule-breakers who go on to deviant careers? To put the question another way, under what conditions is residual rule-breaking stabilized? The conventional hypothesis is that the answer lies in the rule-breaker himself. The hypothesis

32. J. Schwartz and G. L. Baum, "The History of Histoplasmosis," *New England Journal of Medicine*, 256 (1957), pp. 253-258.

suggested here is that the most important single factor
(but not the only factor) in the stabilization of residual
rule-breaking is the societal reaction. Residual rule-
breaking may be stabilized if it is defined to be evidence
of mental illness, and/or the rule-breaker is placed in a
deviant status, and begins to play the role of the mentally ill. In order to avoid the implication that mental
disorder is merely role-playing and pretence, it is necessary to discuss the social institution of insanity in the
next chapter.

3

The Social Institution
of Insanity

AMONG psychiatrists, Szasz has been the most outspoken critic of the use of the medical model when applied to "mental illness." His criticism has taken the form that mental illness is a myth, which serves functions which are largely non-medical in nature:

Our adversaries are not demons, witches, fate, or mental illness. We have no enemy whom we can fight, exorcise, or dispel by "cure." What we do have are *problems in living*—whether these be biologic, economic, political, or sociopsychological. . . . The field to which modern psychiatry addresses itself is vast, and I made no effort to encompass it all. My argument was limited to the proposition that mental illness is a myth, whose function it is to disguise and thus render more palatable the bitter pill of moral conflicts in human relations.[1]

Szasz' formulations of the social, nonmedical functions which the idea of mental illness is made to serve are clear, cogent, and convincing. His conceptualization of the behavior which is symptomatic of "mental illness," however, is open to criticisms of a social-psychological nature.

In the *Myth of Mental Illness*, Szasz proposes that mental disorder be viewed within the framework of "the

1. T. S. Szasz, "The Myth of Mental Illness," *American Psychologist*, 15 (February, 1960), pp. 113-118.

game-playing model of human behavior."² He then describes hysteria, schizophrenia, and other mental disorders as the "impersonation" of sick persons by those
whose "real" problem concerns "problems of living."
Although Szasz states that role-playing by mental patients may not be completely or even mostly voluntary,
the implication is that mental disorder be viewed as a
strategy chosen by the individual as a way of obtaining
help from others. Thus, the term "impersonation" suggests calculated and deliberate shamming by the patient.
Although he notes differences between behavior patterns
of hysteria, malingering, and cheating, he suggests that
these differences may be mostly a matter of whose point
of view is taken in describing the behavior.

INDIVIDUAL AND INTERPERSONAL SYSTEMS
IN ROLE-PLAYING

The present discussion also uses the role-playing
model to analyze mental disorder, but places more emphasis on the involuntary aspects of role-playing than
Szasz, who tends to treat role-playing as an individual
system of behavior. In many social psychological discussions, however, role-playing is considered as a part of a
social system. The individual plays his role by articu-
lating his behavior with the cues and actions of other
persons involved in the transaction. The proper performance of a role is dependent on having a cooperative
audience. The proposition may also be reversed: having
an audience that acts toward the individual in a uniform
way may lead the actor to play the expected role even
if he is not particularly interested in doing so. The "baby
of the family" may come to find this role obnoxious, but

2. Szasz, *op. cit.*

the uniform pattern of cues and actions that confronts him in the family may lock in with his own vocabulary of responses so that it is inconvenient and difficult for him not to play the part expected of him. To the degree that alternative roles are closed off, the proffered role may come to be the only way the individual can cope with the situation.[3]

One of Szasz' very apt formulations touches upon the social systemic aspects of role-playing. He draws an analogy between the role of the mentally ill and the "type-casting" of actors.[4] Some actors get a reputation for playing one type of role, and find it difficult to obtain other roles. Although they may be displeased, they may also come to incorporate aspects of the type-cast role into their self-conceptions, and ultimately into their behavior. Findings in several social psychological studies suggest that an individual's role behavior may be shaped by the kinds of "deference" that he regularly receives from others.[5]

One aspect of the voluntariness of role-playing is the

3. A current definition of social role is "a pattern of behavior associated with a distinctive social position, e.g., that of father, teacher, employer, or patient." L. Broom and P. Selznick, *Sociology* (New York: Harper and Row, 1963), 3rd ed., p. 16.

4. Szasz, *op. cit.* For a discussion of type-casting see O. E. Klapp, *Heroes, Villains and Fools* (Englewood Cliffs, N.J.: Prentice-Hall, 1962), pp. 5-8 *et passim*.

5. Z. S. Blau, "Changes in Status and Age Identification," *American Sociological Review*, 21 (April, 1956), pp. 198-203; J. Benjamins, "Changes in Performance in Relation to Influences upon Self-Conceptualization," *Journal of Abnormal and Social Psychology*, 45 (July, 1950), pp. 473-480; A. Ellis, "The Sexual Psychology of Human Hermaphrodites," *Psychosomatic Medicine*, 7 (March, 1945), pp. 108-125; S. Lieberman, "The Effect of Changes in Roles on the Attitudes of Role Occupants," *Human Relations*, 9 (1956), pp. 385-402. For a review of experimental evidence, see J. H. Mann, "Experimental Evaluations of Role Playing," *Psychological Bulletin*, 53 (May, 1956), pp. 227-234. For an interesting demonstration of the interrelations between symptoms of patients on the same ward, see S. G. Kellam and J. B. Chassan, "Social Context and Symptom Fluctuation," *Psychiatry*, 25 (November, 1962), pp. 370-381.

extent to which the actor believes in the part he is playing. Although a role may be played cynically, with no belief, or completely sincerely, with whole-hearted belief, many roles are played on the basis of an intricate mixture of belief and disbelief. During the course of a study of a large public mental hospital, several patients told the author in confidence about their cynical use of their symptoms—to frighten new personnel, to escape from unpleasant work details, and so on. Yet, at other times, these *same* patients appear to have been sincere in their symptomatic behavior. Apparently it was sometimes difficult for them to tell whether they were playing the role or the role was playing them. Certain types of symptomatology are quite interesting in this connection. In cases of patients simulating previous psychotic states, and in the behavior pattern known to psychiatrists as the Ganser syndrome, it is apparently almost impossible for the observer to separate feigning of symptoms from involuntary acts with any degree of certainty.

The following case history excerpt will illustrate what psychiatrists have called simulation of a previous psychotic state:

A 32-year-old white man, an engineer, was readmitted to the hospital because of the recurrence of psychotic behavior. He had been hospitalized twice previously. The first time he had had electroshock treatment and had a remission for 4 years. One of us . . . saw him during his second hospitalization. At that time he was severely regressed, hallucinating freely, had magical and delusional behavior and many ideas of a Messianic nature. He made a good functional recovery after several months of intensive psychotherapy by his private psychiatrist, supplemented with insulin coma treatment. Several years later he had a recurrence of symptoms and, because of my acquaintance with him during the previous hospitalization, he was referred by his previous therapist. On admission his behavior was bizarre enough to warrant sending him to the disturbed unit. There he immediately took over the unit claiming seniority rights because of his previous stay. When seen he was jovially patronizing, referred to his voices in a smiling manner and interspersed the interview with vague magical inferences of seemingly great significance. He continually made a particular gesture, that of a clock with the hands at the 6 o'clock position. This gesture had been the subject of much inquiry and work on his previous admission. As a result of the prior contact, it was possible to be more direct and enquiring with him than if he had been a new patient. At this point he gave no indications as to the precipitating stimulus of disruptive conflict. During some bantering in which he referred to his current hospitalization as a vacation, or a return of the old grad to his Alma Mater, he was told that this might prove to be an expensive class reunion. (This was in reference to one of his ostensible reasons for discontinuing psychotherapy following his previous disorder, namely, that treatment was too costly.) With almost dramatic swiftness following this remark, his bizarre behavior stopped and he became quite depressed although still communicative. The following day it was possible to transfer him to a less controlled unit and he described in a completely coherent fashion with intense but appropriate emotion that he was extremely angry with his wife for nagging and belittling him. He was afraid he would not be able to control himself and felt that if he were sick like the last time he could avoid a feared outburst of physical violence by being hospitalized. In a few days he was able to recognize that much of the rage at his wife was directed at her current pregnancy. Although a moderate depression persisted, there was no recurrence of the bizarre behavior or the apparent hallucinations. He left the hospital after 3 weeks and returned directly to his job and home.[6]

6. L. Sadow and A. Suslick, "Simulation of a Previous Psychotic State," *A.M.A. Archives of General Psychiatry*, 4 (May, 1961), pp. 452-458.

What makes "simulation" particularly relevant to a social systemic theory of mental illness is that it is believed that such behavior is usually a defensive reaction to external stress:

[This condition] consists of varying degrees of conscious simulation of the previous psychotic state by and under the control of the patient's ego when a subsequent situation of stress occurs.[7]

This psychiatric definition closely parallels Lemert's sociological definition of "secondary deviation":

When a person begins to employ his deviant behavior or a role based upon it as a means of defense, attack, or adjustment to the overt and covert problems created by the consequent societal reaction, his deviation is secondary.[8]

Moreover, it appears that such simulation can occur even where there has been no previous psychotic episode:

A particularly striking example of this was seen in a young hospital record custodian who developed a complex of subjective symptoms highly suggestive of a frontal lobe brain tumor. Laboratory and physical tests short of air studies had revealed that her difficulties were of a conversion-like nature and were in part patterned after case histories which she had read with more diligence than called for by her job.[9]

Apparently one can play the role of a mentally ill person without ever having actually experienced the role. Vicarious learning of imagery of the role of the mentally ill will be discussed below, in the section following Proposition 5.

The Ganser syndrome appears to illustrate the intricate manner in which voluntary and involuntary ele-

7. *Ibid.*, p. 452.
8. Lemert, *op. cit.*, p. 76.
9. Sadow and Suslick, *op. cit.*, p. 453.

ments intertwine in role-playing. This condition is referred to by psychiatrists as the "approximate answer" or *Vorbeireden* (talking past the point) syndrome:

The patient is disoriented as to time and space and gives absurd answers to questions. Often he claims he does not know who he is, where he comes from, or where he is. When he is asked to do simple calculations, he makes obvious mistakes—for instance, giving 5 as the sum of 2 plus 2. When he is asked to identify objects, he gives the name of a related object. Upon being shown scissors, the patient may say they are knives; a picture of a dog may be identified as a cat, a yellow object may be called red, and so on. If he is asked what a hammer is used for, he may reply to cut wood. If he is shown a dime, he may state that it is a half dollar and so on. If he is asked how many legs a horse has, he may reply, "Six."

At times almost a game seems to go on between the examiner and the patient. The examiner asks questions which are almost silly in their simplicity, but the patient succeeds in giving a sillier answer. And yet it seems that the patient understands the question, because the answer, although wrong, is related to the question.[10]

In accordance with what has been said here about the social systemic nature of role-playing, the difficulty in interpreting simulation of previous psychotic states, and the Ganser syndrome, is that the patient is just as confused by his own behavior as is the observer.

Some psychiatrists suspect that in schizophrenia there is a large element of behavior that is in the borderline zone between volitional and non-volitional activity. Here are some excerpts from an aubiographical account of schizophrenia which stress the role-playing aspects:

10. S. Arieti and J. M. Meth, "Rare, Unclassifiable, Collective and Exotic Psychotic Syndromes," in S. Arieti (ed.), *American Handbook of Psychiatry* (New York: Basic Books, 1959), Vol. 1, p. 547.

We schizophrenics say and do a lot of stuff that is unimportant, and then we mix important things in with all this to see if the doctor cares enough to see them and feel them. . . .

Patients laugh and posture when they see through the doctor who says he will help but really won't or can't . . . They try to please the doctor but also confuse him so he won't go into anything important. When you find people who will really help, you don't need to distract them. You can act in a normal way.

I can sense if the doctor not only wants to help but also can and will help. . . .

Patients kick and scream and fight when they aren't sure the doctor can see them. It's a most terrifying feeling to realize that the doctor can't understand what you feel and that he's just going ahead with his own ideas. I would start to feel that I was invisible or maybe not there at all. I had to make an uproar to see if the doctor would respond to me, not just his own ideas.[11]

Note that this patient has applied to herself a deviant label ("we schizophrenics") and that her behavior fits Lemert's definition of secondary deviation; she appears to have used the deviant role as a means of adjustment.

This discussion suggests that a stable role performance may arise when the actor's role imagery locks in with the type of "deference" which he regularly receives. An extreme example of this process may be taken from anthropological and medical reports concerning the "dead role," as in deaths attributed to "bone-pointing." Death from bone-pointing appears to arise from the conjunction of two fundamental processes that characterize all social behavior. First, all individuals continually orient

11. M. L. Hayward and J. E. Taylor, "A Schizophrenic Patient Describes the Action of Intensive Psychotherapy," *The Psychiatric Quarterly*, 30 (1956), p. 211.

themselves by means of responses that are perceived in social interaction: the individual's identity and continuity of experience are dependent on these cues. Generalizing from experimental findings, Blake and Mouton make this statement about the processes of conformity, resistance to influence, and conversion to a new role:

An individual requires a stable framework, including salient and firm reference points, in order to orient himself and to regulate his interactions with others. This framework consists of external and internal anchorages available to the individual whether he is aware of them or not. With an acceptable framework he can resist giving or accepting information that is inconsistent with that framework or that requires him to relinquish it. In the absence of a stable framework he actively seeks to establish one through his own strivings by making use of significant and relevant information provided within the context of interaction. By controlling the amount and kind of information available for orientation, he can be led to embrace conforming attitudes which are entirely foreign to his earlier ways of thinking.[12]

Secondly, the individual has his own vocabulary of expectations, which may in a particular situation either agree with or be in conflict with the sanctions to which he is exposed. Entry into a role may be complete when this role is part of the individual's expectations, and when these expectations are reaffirmed in social interaction. In the following pages this principle will be

12. R. R. Blake and J. S. Mouton, "Conformity, Resistance and Conversion," in I. A. Berg and B. M. Bass (eds.), *Conformity and Deviation* (New York: Harper, 1961), pp. 1-2. For a recent and striking demonstration of the effect of social communication in defining internal stimuli, see S. Schachter and J. E. Singer, "Cognitive, Social and Physiological Determinants of Emotional State," *Psychological Review*, 69 (September, 1962), pp. 379-399.

applied to the problem of the causation of mental disorder, through considerations of the social institution of insanity.

LEARNING AND MAINTAINING ROLE-IMAGERY

What are the beliefs and practices that constitute the social institution of insanity? And how do they figure in the development of mental disorder? Two propositions concerning beliefs about mental disorder in the general public will now be considered.

4. *Stereotyped imagery of mental disorder is learned in early childhood.* Although there are no substantiating studies in this area, scattered observations lead the author to conclude that children learn a considerable amount of imagery concerning deviance very early, and that much of the imagery comes from their peers rather than from adults. The literal meaning of "crazy," a term now used in a wide variety of contexts, is probably grasped by children during the first years of elementary school. Since adults are often vague and evasive in their responses to questions in this area, an aura of mystery surrounds it. In this socialization the grossest stereotypes that are heir to childhood fears, e.g., of the "boogie man," survive. These conclusions are quite speculative, of course, and need to be investigated systematically, possibly with techniques similar to those used in studies of the early learning of racial stereotypes.

Here are some psychiatric observations on "playing crazy" in a group of child patients. This material indicates that the social stereotypes are held by these children (ages 8-12) and play an active part in their cognition and behavior. It also fits the preceding discussion of role-playing and secondary deviation.

Equally prominent are their intense concerns about craziness, about the possibility that *they themselves* are crazy. . . . This concern seems to reflect the children's response to their own sporadic psychotic experience and behavior, a social awareness of how they appear to others, and perhaps in a sense an attempt to "explain" their own behavior. Undoubtedly, they are also reacting to teasing and name-calling by peers, and exasperated remarks by parents and teachers. . . .

The child's concern about being crazy obtrudes in many different ways and places. Malcolm, in associating to his figure drawing, perseverates remarks about craziness: "He's a crazy person," "He doesn't have a mind, just a nut," "A nut, that's the way he is, he was born that way," "She's nuts, that's what people say about her—Hitler was nuts, wasn't he?" Gale enters her therapist's office obviously upset, abruptly refuses to talk of any worries, insists she's fine. Soon she tells of seeing a sign in the waiting room about lectures on emotionally disturbed children, and she cries out that she's not crazy. Bob accidentally cuts his finger in the occupational therapy shop. Badly shaking, he stares at the blood and yells, "My God, I'm going crazy." Another talks of only wanting Looney Tunes comics: "Looney Tunes," he snorts, "that's for me all right." Mark finds he has confused his craft shop days, is afraid that this means he's losing his mind. Many of the children use humor about or project these concerns . . . describing . . . other people as "crazy." They often focus their craziness, with or without past neurological exams and EEG's, upon their brain—"Got no brain," "My brain is loose and swims around in my head," "My brain and mind are no good, they get tired too quick," "Sometimes I get—it feels like explosions in my head," "Something snaps up there."

. . . A considerable component of the erratic behavior of these

children has a conscious element—that is, they are "playing crazy."
Much, though by no means all, of the playing crazy centers around
their past experiences of and continual concerns about "being
crazy." Their playing crazy takes many forms. It may be very
quiet and subtle or blatant and obvious, identified as "pretend"
by the child or exhaustively "defended" as crazy. Some of the
varied forms are: "looking odd," staring off into space, or acting
utterly confused; wild, primitive, disorganized ragelike states; odd
verbalizations, incoherencies, mutterings; alleged hallucinations
and delusions; the child's insistence that he is an animal, goblin,
or other creature; or various grossly bizarre behaviors. Most of the
children show many of these forms of playing crazy. Most of the
children make clear—though by no means reliable—annonncements
that they have played crazy or intend to do so, or speak of "just
pretending." The complex components of their playing crazy often
become clear only after extended observation and therapeutic work.

At times, the child is quite consciously, deliberately, almost
zestfully playing crazy—he is under no significant internal pressure,
is completely in control, and at the end is most reassured. For
if one can openly *pretend* to be crazy, how can one really be
crazy? Not only current concerns but actual past incidents may
thus be magically wiped away. Perhaps more frequently, playing
crazy is used as other types of play are often used, namely, to
achieve belated mastery of traumatic events, or anxiety-provoking
internal states. . . .

At still other times—again *not* when under much pressure or
anywhere near disintegration—the children pretend or toy with
craziness, in a deliberate and controlled manner, as if they were
almost experimenting with or testing attenuated psychotic experiences: the behavior somehow seems directed toward mastery of
anticipated states rather than toward reduction of old anxieties.
One feels that the child is saying, "What if such-and-such should
happen. . . ?." or "What would it be like if . . .?" It might well
be labeled an "antisurprise" measure, though clearly the previous
psychotic states are not totally unrelated to this form of behavior,

in which the child tentatively feels his way into feared future experiences of disintegration. Fenichel puts it well: ". . . a test action: repeating the overwhelming past and anticipating the possible future." Tensions are created, ". . . which *might* occur, but at a time and in a degree which is determined by the participant himself, and which is therefore under control."

At other times, when slipping toward or virtually in a psychotic state, the children may still attempt in a frenzied fashion to pretend to be crazy. Or perhaps more accurately, they pretend to be *crazier* than they are at that moment. . . .

Sometimes the child keeps a sharp eye on his audience's reaction while producing a quite contrived, controlled production of craziness. He fretfully awaits a response as he asks an observer to define him. "*Am* I insane? Do *you* think I'm so insane, so out of control that I could *really* . . . behave this way?" Should the response be oversolicitous, he may be badly threatened by the possibility that he *is* what he fears and pretends to be. And he may angrily plead, as did Bart on such occasions, "I'm not *that* crazy!"[13]
[Footnotes omitted]

Assuming that hypothesis #4 is sound, what effect does early learning have on the shared conceptions of insanity held in the community? In early childhood much fallacious material is learned that is later discarded when more adequate information replaces it. This question leads to Hypothesis 5.

5. *The stereotypes of insanity are continually reaffirmed, inadvertently, in ordinary social interaction.* Although many adults become acquainted with medical concepts of mental illness, the traditional stereotypes are not discarded, but continue to exist alongside the medical conceptions, because the stereotypes receive almost

13. A. C. Cain, "On the Meaning of 'Playing Crazy' in Borderline Children," *Psychiatry*, 27 (August, 1964), pp. 278-289. The quotation is from pp. 280-282.

continual support from the mass media and in ordinary social discourse. In mental health education campaigns, televised lectures by psychiatrists and others, magazine articles and newspaper feature stories, medical discussions of mental illness occur from time to time. These types of discussions, however, seem to be far outnumbered by stereotypic references.

A recent study by Nunnally demonstrates that the portrait of mental illness in mass media is highly stereotyped. In a systematic and large-scale content analysis of television, radio, newspapers, and magazines, he found an image of mental disorder presented which was overwhelmingly stereotyped.

Media presentations emphasized the bizarre symptoms of the mentally ill. For example, information relating to factor I (the conception that mentally ill persons look and act different from 'normal' people) was recorded 89 times. Of these, 88 affirm the factor, that is, indicated or suggested that people with mental health problems "look and act different:" only one item denied factor I. In television dramas, for example, the afflicted person often enters the scene staring glassy-eyed, with his mouth widely ajar, mumbling incoherent phrases or laughing uncontrollably. Even in what would be considered the milder disorders, neurotic phobias and obsessions, the afflicted person is presented as having bizarre facial expressions and actions.[14]

Of particular interest are the comparisons made between the imagery of mental disorder in the mass media, among mental health experts, and in the general public. In addition to the mass media analysis, data were collected from a group of psychiatrists and psychologists, and from a sample drawn from the total population. The

---

14. J. C. Nunnally, Jr., *Popular Conceptions of Mental Health* (New York: Holt, Rinehart and Winston, 1961), p. 74.

comparisons are summarized in a table which is reproduced below.[15]

The solid line, representing the responses of the

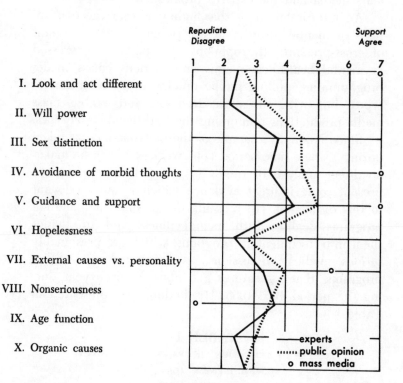

FIGURE 1[15]

COMPARISONS OF EXPERTS, THE PUBLIC, AND THE MASS MEDIA
ON THE 10 INFORMATION FACTORS

mental health experts, lies furthest to the left, in the direction of least stereotypy. The small circles—summarizing the findings in the study of the mass media—lie, for

15. *Idem.*

the most part, to the extreme right, the direction of greatest stereotypy. The broken line, indicating the findings of the sample survey in the public, lies between the mass media and the expert's profiles.

An interpretation of this finding is that the conceptions of mental disorder in the public are the resultant of cross-pressure: the opinions of experts, as expressed in mental health campaigns and "serious" mass media programming, pulling public opinion away from stereotypes, but with the more frequent and visible mass media productions reinforcing the traditional stereotypes.

Since Nunnally's sample of the mass media was taken during a single time period (one week of 1955), he makes no direct analysis of trends in time. However, he does present some indirect evidence which is quite relevant to this discussion. He presents the number of television programs dealing with mental illness and subdivides them into documentary programs, which are presumably serious medical discussions, as contrasted with other programs; that is, features and films for each year during the period 1951-1958. His findings are presented in Table 1.

TABLE 1

NUMBER OF TELEVISION PROGRAMS DEALING WITH
MENTAL ILLNESS, 1951-58[16]

	1951–53	1954	1955
Documentary programs	4	15	2
Other (features and films)	1	12	37

	1956	1957	1958
Documentary programs	2	1	1
Other (features and films)	122	169	72

16. *Ibid.*, p. 79.

Once again we see in a recent period (1957-1958) that the other features outnumber the serious programs with a ratio of the order of 100 to 1. Apparently, moreover, this disproportion was not decreasing, as many mental health workers believed, but actually increasing, as popular interest in mental disorder increases.

Although Nunnally's study represents a contribution to our knowledge of the imagery in the mass media and the general public, it is somewhat limited in terms of our present discussion, because the study deals only with direct references to mental illness, and uses an incomplete set of categories for evaluating the references. The set of categories will be discussed first: direct references are discussed below.

The categories that are used in evaluating the content of the imagery of mental illness are of unequal interest; Categories 1—"look and act different"—and 6—"hopelessness"—are probably essential in understanding the mental illness imagery in the general public. There are other dimensions, however, which are not included in Nunnally's analysis, the most important of which are dangerousness, unpredictability, and negative evaluation. This can be made clear by referring to newspaper coverage of mental illness.

In newspapers it is a common practice to mention that a rapist or a murderer was once a mental patient. Here are several examples: Under the headline "Question Girl in Child Slaying," the story begins, "A 15-year-old girl *with a history of mental illness* is being questioned in connection with a kidnap-slaying of a 3-year-old boy." A similar story under the headline "Man Killed, Two Policemen Hurt in Hospital Fray," begins "*A former mental patient* grabbed a policeman's revolver and began shooting at 15 persons in the receiving room of City Hospital No. 2 Thursday."

Often acts of violence will be connected with mental illness on the basis of little or no evidence. For instance, under the headline "Milwaukee Man Goes Berserk, Shoots Officer," the story describes the events and then quotes a police captain who said, "He may be a mental case." In another story, under the headline, "Texas Dad Kills Self, Four Children, Daughter Says," the last sentence of the story is "One report said Kinsey (the killer) was once a mental patient." In most large newspapers there apparently is at least one such story in every issue.

Even if the coverage of these acts of violence was highly accurate, it would still give the reader a misleading impression because negative information is seldom offset by positive reports. An item like the following is almost inconceivable:

Mrs. Ralph Jones, an ex-mental patient, was elected president of the Fairview Home and Garden Society at their meeting last Thursday.

Because of highly biased reporting, the reader is free to make the unwarranted inference that murder and rape and other acts of violence occur more frequently among former mental patients than among the population at large. Actually it has been demonstrated that the incidence of crimes of violence (or of any crime) is much lower among former mental patients than in the general population.[17] Yet, because of newspaper practice, this is

17. H. Brill and B. Malzberg, *Statistical Report Based on the Arrest Record of 5,354 Ex-patients Released from New York State Mental Hospitals During the Period 1946-1948* (Available from the authors). See also L. H. Cohen and H. Freeman, "How Dangerous to the Community are State Hospital Patients?" *Connecticut State Medical Journal*, 9 (September, 1945), pp. 697-700; D. W. Hastings, "Follow-up Results in Psychiatric Illness," *American Journal of Psychiatry*, 114 (June, 1958), pp. 1057-66; J. R. Rappeport *et al.*, "Evaluation and Follow-up of State Hospital Patients Who Had Sanity Hearings," *American Journal of Psychiatry*, 118 (June, 1962), pp. 1078-86. Suicide is an impor-

not the picture presented to the public. Newspapers have established an ineluctable relationship between mental illness and violence. Perhaps as importantly, this connection also signifies the incurability of mental disorder; that is, it connects *former* mental patients with violent and unpredictable acts.

It seems paradoxical that progress in communication techniques has created a situation in which the stereotyping process is probably growing stronger. Newspapers now use teletype release from the press associations; and since these associations report incidents of crime and violence involving mental patients from the entire nation, the sampling bias in the picture presented to the public is enormous.

There are approximately 600,000 adults confined to mental hospitals in the United States on any one day, and an even larger group of former mental patients. The newspaper practice of daily reporting the violent acts of some patient, or former patient, and at the same time, seldom indicating the size of the vast group of nonviolent patients, is grossly misleading. Inadvertently, newspapers use selective reporting of the same type that is found in the most blatantly false advertisements and propaganda, to continually "prove" that mental patients are unpredictably violent.

The impact of selective reportage is great because it confirms the public's stereotypes of insanity. Even if

tant exception to these findings. The rate of suicide is reported in a number of studies as considerably higher among patients and ex-patients than among the rest of the population. Even though the relative rate is high, the absolute rate is still quite low. For example, a recent study reports a suicide rate of 1.65 per cent for patients and ex-patients of the psychiatric service of a Texas VA Hospital, as compared with 0.23 for a comparable non-patient group (A. D. Pokorny, "Suicide Rates in Various Psychiatric Disorders," *Journal of Nervous and Mental Disease*, 139 [December, 1964], pp. 499-506). W. O. Hagstrom suggested this exception to me.

the newspaper were to explain the bias in these stories, the problem would not be eliminated. The vivid portrayal of a single case of human violence has more emotional impact on the reader than the statistics which indicate the true actuarial risks from mental patients as a class.

The average person's reaction to the fact that the probability of the kind of violence that the newspapers report occurring is about one in a million, is usually that this is still a real risk which he will not accept. Yet this is roughly the risk of death he unthinkingly accepts in taking a cross-country trip in an airplane or automobile. One component of the stereotype of insanity is an unreasoned and unreasonable fear of mental patients which makes the public reluctant to take risks in this area of the same size as risks frequently encountered and accepted in the ordinary round of living.

Reaffirmation of the stereotype of insanity occurs not only in the mass media but indirectly in ordinary conversation: in jokes, anecdotes, and even in conventional phrases. Such phrases as "are you crazy?" or "it would be a madhouse," or "it's driving me out of my mind," or "we were chatting like crazy," or "he was running like mad," and literally hundreds of others occur frequently in informal conversations. In this usage, insanity itself is seldom the topic of conversation, and the discussants do not mean to refer to the topic of insanity, and are usually unaware that they are doing so.

I have overheard mental patients, when talking among themselves, using these phrases unthinkingly. Even those mental health workers, such as psychiatrists, psychologists, and social workers, who are most interested in changing the concept of mental disorder often use these terms—sometimes jokingly but usually unthinkingly—in their informal discussions. These terms are so

FIGURE 2

VISUAL AND VERBAL IMAGERY ABOUT MENTAL ILLNESS
Clippings from newspapers and magazines

much a part of ordinary language that only the person who considers every word carefully can eliminate them from his speech. Through verbal usage, the stereotype of insanity is an inflexible part of the social structure.

The imagery which is implicit in these phrases should be discussed. When the phrase "running like mad" is used, the imagery which this conveys implicitly is movement of a wild and perhaps uncontrolled variety. The question "Are you out of your mind?" signifies a behavior of which the speaker disapproves. The frequently used term "crazy," often, although not always, implies subtle ridicule or stigma. These implications are there even when the person using the terms does not mean the words to convey this.

This inadvertent and incidental imagery is similar to that contained in racial and ethnic stereotypes. A speaker who uses the phrase, "Jew a man down," may not necessarily be prejudiced against Jews (as in the rural South, where Jews are rare), but simply uses the phrase as a matter of convenience in order to convey his meaning, but to others the assumptions are unmistakable—the image of the Jew as a person who is scheming and over-interested in money for its own sake.

Again as in racial and ethnic stereotypes, imagery is sometimes conveyed through jokes and anecdotes.[18] An example of the type of joke which one hears in informal conversation is taken from the *Reader's Digest:*

A visitor to a mental hospital sees a patient who looks and acts like a normal person. He asks him why he is in the hospital. "Because I like potato pancakes," the patient replies. The visitor

18. For references to the use of humor as an instrument of social control, see R. Middleton and J. Moland, "Humor in Negro and White Subcultures: A Study of Jokes Among University Students," *American Sociological Review,* 24 (February, 1959), pp. 61-69.

says, "That's nothing, I like potato pancakes myself." The patient turns to the visitor excitedly, "You do!" he replies, "Why don't you come to my room then, I have a whole trunkfull!"

The implications that one might draw from this type of joke are fairly clear. Persons who are mentally ill, even when they do not seem to be, are basically different. This is one theme, among others, which recurs in reference to mental illness in ordinary conversation. This theme, together with the "looks and acts different" theme and the "incurable" theme, is probably part of a single larger pattern: these deviants (like other deviants) belong to a fundamentally different class of human beings, or perhaps even a different species. This is a manifestation of out-grouping, the beliefs and actions that are based on the premise that one's enemies, strangers, or deviants, no matter how attractive or sympathetic they might seem to the unwary, are essentially and fundamentally different than one's own kind.

A racial joke will provide an illustration of this genre, the fundamental difference and inferiority, of the out-group:

A Negro advertising executive is interviewed in his home, a luxurious apartment on the Hudson, on the television program Person-to-Person. He is impeccably dressed, articulate, and speaks with the easy, cultivated accents of East Coast society. He says, "Good evening Ed." Murrow says, "Good evening, Mr. Johnson." The executive introduces his family. Murrow says, "Before you take us on a tour of your home, could you tell our audience something about your working day? Mr. Johnson says, "Certainly, Ed. On the typical weekday, my man comes around to pick me up about 9, and we get to the Avenue about 10. I have an accounts conference until 12, lunch and cocktails till 2. At 2 another accounts conference until 4, then I dictate letters until about 6. My man picks me up, I'm home by 7. As often as not, we have people over for dinner and drinks. They stay until 11 or 12, then I go out on the balcony, and *jes look out ober de ribber*."

To summarize this section: public stereotypes of mental illness are difficult to change because they receive continual although inadvertent support from the mass media and in ordinary conversation. In support of this proposition, evidence from several studies and the author's observations have been cited.

On the basis of this evidence one would suspect that mental health campaigns which are based largely on disseminating information will be doomed to failure because of the overwhelming preponderance of stereotyped information and imagery to which the average person is exposed.

It is difficult to say at this time how the situation could be changed. In some media, TV for example, a definite attempt is made to "clean up" the references to mental illness. As Nunnally points out, however, these attempts are not particularly successful.[19] While television has managed to eliminate virtually all the irreverent slang references to mental illness such as "goof ball," "flipped," "nut," and "loony," there has been no attempt to change the visual imagery.

Why are these stereotypes resistant to change? One possible explanation is that they are functional for the current social order and tend to be integrated into the psychological make-up of all members of the society. Racial stereotypes may perform similar functions. In the southern part of the United States, for example, racial stereotypes are not fortuitous and isolated attitudes; rather, they are integral parts of the southerner's cognitive structure. The stereotype of the Negro fulfills the

19. Nunnally, *op. cit.*, p. 86.

functions of a contrast conception, a reference point for making social comparisons and self-evaluations. One clue to the existence of contrast conceptions is a highly proliferated vocabulary of vernacular terms, such as exists in the South for referral to Negroes. Jig, coon, spade, buck, and jungle bunny are only a few of an enormous number of such terms. In current vernacular, there is an equally large number of terms for referring to insanity, or going insane; a few specimens are: out of one's mind, or losing one's mind, or the mind snapping, out of one's head, wrong in the head, not right in the head, (or a gesture in which one moves the finger in a circle while pointing to one's head), teched in the head, cracked, loony, off one's rocker, off the deep end, nuts, bughouse, flipped, psycho, goofy, ga-ga, lose your marbles, bats in the belfry (or just "bats"), screwy or screwball, crazy, deranged, demented, and others.

Judging from the frequency with which references to mental disorder appear in the mass media and in colloquial speech, the concept of mental disorder serves as a fundamental contrast conception in our society, functioning to preserve the current mores. The displacement of such a convenient concept is probably resisted for this reason. In some preliterate societies, the concept of spirit possession "explains" dreams, sickness, mental disorder, great success, untimely death, and many otherwise unexplainable phenomena. The average member of such a society has, therefore, a substantial psychological investment in the belief in spirit possession.

Similarly, in the United States, the average citizen resists changes in his concept of insanity—or, if he is in the middle class, his concept of mental disease—because these concepts are functional for maintaining his customary moral and cognitive world.

This section will be concluded with a discussion of

a process which may relate stereotyping of the mentally ill to the social dynamics of mental illness: vicarious learning. The transmission of stereotyped imagery in the mass media and ordinary conversation may throw light on a question that has been hotly debated; whether the symptoms of mental disorder are inherent or learned. Although advocates of the learning point of view have pointed to instances where symptoms seemed to be learned (*folie à deux*, role models in the family), they have never been completely satisfied with this explanation, since it places so much emphasis on what seems to be infrequent occurrences.

The discussion here suggests that *everyone* in a society learns the symptoms of mental disorder vicariously, through the imagery that is conveyed, unintentionally, in everyday life. This imagery tends to be tied to the vernacular of each language and culture; this association may be one reason why there are considerable variations in the symptoms of mental disorder that occur in different cultures. If, as suggested here, this imagery is available to the rule-breaker to structure and thus to "understand" his own experience, the quality of the societal reaction becomes extremely important in determining the duration and outcome of the initially amorphous and unstructured residual rule-breaking. The nature of the societal reaction will be shown in the next section to be made up of alternative, indeed, mutually exclusive components—denial or labeling.

DENIAL AND LABELING

According to the analysis presented here, the traditional stereotypes of mental disorder are solidly entrenched in the population because they are learned early in childhood and are continuously reaffirmed in the mass media and in everyday conversation. How do these beliefs function in the processes leading to mental disorder? This question will be considered by first referring to the earlier discussion of the societal reaction to residual rule-breaking.

It was stated that the usual reaction to residual rule-breaking is denial, and that in these cases most rule-breaking is transitory. The societal reaction to rule-breaking is not always denial, however. In a small proportion of cases the reaction goes the other way, exaggerating and at times distorting the extent and degree of the violation. This pattern of exaggeration, which we will call "labeling," has been noted by Garfinkel in his discussion of the "degradation" of officially recognized criminals.[20] Goffman makes a similar point in his description of the "discrediting" of mental patients.

(The patient's case record) is apparently not regularly used to record occasions when the patient showed capacity to cope honorably and effectively with difficult life situations. Nor is the case record typically used to provide a rough average or sampling of his past conduct. (Rather, it extracts) from his whole life course a list of those incidents that have or might have had "symptomatic" significance. . . . I think that most of the information gathered in case records is quite true, although it might seem also to be true that almost anyone's life course could yield up enough denigrating facts to provide grounds for the record's justification of commitment.[21]

Apparently under some conditions the societal reaction to rule-breaking is to seek out signs of abnormality in

20. H. Garfinkel, "Conditions of Successful Degradation Ceremonies," *American Journal of Sociology*, 61 (March, 1956), pp. 420-424.
21. Goffman, "The Moral Career of the Mental Patient," in *Asylums, op. cit.*, pp. 155-56, 159.

the deviant's history to show that he was always essentially a deviant.

The contrasting social reactions of denial and labeling provides a means of answering two fundamental questions. First, if rule-breaking arises from diverse sources —physical, psychological, and situational—how does the uniformity of behavior that is associated with insanity develop? Second, if rule-breaking is usually transitory, how does it become stabilized in those patients who became chronically deviant? To summarize, what are the sources of uniformity and stability of deviant behavior?

In the approach taken here the answer to this question is based on Hypotheses 4 and 5, that the role imagery of insanity is learned early in childhood and is reaffirmed in social interaction. In a crisis, when the deviance of an individual becomes a public issue, the traditional stereotype of insanity becomes the guiding imagery for action, both for those reacting to the deviant and, at times, for the deviant himself. When societal agents and persons around the deviant react to him uniformly in terms of the traditional stereotypes of insanity, his amorphous and unstructured rule-breaking tends to crystallize in conformity to these expectations, thus becoming similar to the behavior of other deviants classified as mentally ill, and stable over time. The process of becoming uniform and stable is completed when the traditional imagery becomes a part of the deviant's orientation for guiding his own behavior.

The idea that cultural stereotypes may stabilize residual rule-breaking and tend to produce uniformity in symptoms, is supported by cross-cultural studies of mental disorder. Although some observers insist there are underlying similarities, many agree that there are enormous differences in the manifest symptoms of stable mental disorder *between* societies, and great similarity *within* societies.[22]

These considerations suggest that the labeling process is a crucial contingency in most careers of residual deviance. Thus Glass, who observed that neuropsychiatric casualties may not become mentally ill if they are kept with their unit, goes on to say that military experience with psychotherapy has been disappointing. Soldiers who are removed from their unit to a hospital, he states, often go on to become chronically impaired.[23] That is, their deviance is stabilized by the labeling process, which is implicit in their removal and hospitalization. A similar interpretation can be made by comparing the observations of childhood disorders among Mexican-Americans with those of "Anglo" children. Childhood disorders such as *susto* (an illness believed to result from fright) sometimes have damaging outcomes in Mexican-American children.[24] Yet the deviant behavior involved is very similar to that which seems to have high incidence among Anglo children, with permanent impairment virtually never occurring. Apparently through cues from his elders the Mexican-American child, behaving initially much like his Anglo counterpart, learns to enter the sick role, at times with serious consequences.[25]

22. P. M. Yap, "Mental Diseases Peculiar to Certain Cultures: A Survey of Comparative Psychiatry," *Journal of Mental Science*, 97 (April, 1951), pp. 313-327.

23. Glass, *op. cit.* For a contrary view, See E. Ginzberg, *The Ineffective Soldier* (New York: Columbia University Press, 1959).

24. L. Saunders, *Cultural Difference and Medical Care* (New York: Russell Sage Foundation, 1954), p. 142.

25. For discussion, with many illustrative cases, of the process in which persons play the "dead role" and subsequently die, see C. C. Herbert, "Life-Influencing Interactions," in A. Simon *et al* (eds.), *The Physiology of the Emotions* (Springfield, Ill.: Charles C Thomas, 1961).

ACCEPTANCE OF THE DEVIANT ROLE

From this point of view, most mental disorder can be considered to be a social role. This social role complements and reflects the status of the insane in the social structure. It is through the social processes which maintain the status of the insane that the varied rule-breaking from which mental disorder arises is made uniform and stable. The stabilization and uniformization of residual deviance are completed when the deviant accepts the role of the insane as the framework within which he organizes his own behavior. Three hypotheses are stated below which suggest some of the processes which cause the deviant to accept such a stigmatized role.

6. *Labeled deviants may be rewarded for playing the stereotyped deviant role.* Ordinarily patients who display "insight" are rewarded by psychiatrists and other personnel. That is, patients who manage to find evidence of "their illness" in their past and present behavior, confirming the medical and societal diagnosis, receive benefits. This pattern of behavior is a special case of a more general pattern that has been called the "apostolic function" by Balint, in which the physician and others inadvertently cause the patient to display symptoms of the illness the physician thinks the patient has. The apostolic function occurs in the context of bargaining between the patient and the doctor over what shall be decided to be the nature of the patient's illness:

Some of the people who, for some reason or other, find it difficult to cope with problems of their lives resort to becoming ill. If the doctor has the opportunity of seeing them in the first phases of their being ill, i.e. before they settle down to a definite "organized" illness, he may observe that these patients, so to speak, offer or propose various illnesses, and that they have to go on offering new illnesses until between doctor and patient an agreement can be reached resulting in the acceptance by both of them of one of the illnesses as justified.[26]

It is in this fluid situation that Balint believes the doctor influences the manifestations of illness:

Apostolic mission or function means in the first place that every doctor has a vague, but almost unshakably firm, idea of how a patient ought to behave when ill. Although this idea is anything but explicit and concrete, it is immensely powerful, and influences, as we have found, practically every detail of the doctor's work with his patients. *It was almost as if every doctor had revealed knowledge of what was right and what was wrong for patients to expect and to endure, and further, as if he had a sacred duty to convert to his faith all the ignorant and unbelieving among his patients.*[27]

Not only physicians but other hospital personnel and even other patients, reward the deviant for conforming to the stereotypes. Caudill, who made observations of ward life in the guise of being a patient, reports various pressures from fellow patients. In the following excerpt, for example, there is the suggestion in the advice of the other patients that he should realize that he is a sick man:

On the second day, following a conference with his therapist, the observer expressed resentment over not having going-out privileges to visit the library and work on his book—his compulsive concern over his inability to finish this task being (according to his simulated case history) one of the factors leading to his hospitalization. Immediately two patients, Mr. Hill and Mrs. Lewis, who were

26. Balint, *op. cit.*, p. 18.
27. *Ibid.*, p. 216.

later to become his closest friends, told him he was being "defensive"; since his doctor did not wish him to do such work, it was probably better "to lay off it." Mr. Hill went on to say that one of his troubles when he first came to the hospital was thinking of things that he had to do or thought he had to do. He said that now he did not bother about anything. Mrs. Lewis said that at first she had treated the hospital as a sort of hotel and had spent her therapeutic hours "charming" her doctor, but it had been pointed out to her by others that this was a mental hospital and that she should actively work with her doctor if she expected to get well.[28]

In the California mental hospital in which the author conducted a study in 1959, a common theme in the discussions between patients on the admissions wards was the "recognition" of one's illness. This interchange, which took place during a ward meeting on a female admission ward, provides an extreme example:

NEW PATIENT: "I don't belong here. I don't like all these crazy people. When can I talk to the doctor? I've been here four days and I haven't seen the doctor. I'm not crazy."

ANOTHER PATIENT: "She says she's not crazy." (Laughter from patients.)

ANOTHER PATIENT: "Honey, what I'd like to know is, if you're not crazy, how did you get your ass in this hospital?"

NEW PATIENT: "It's complicated, but I can explain. My husband and I. . . ."

FIRST PATIENT: "That's what they all say." (General Laughter.)

Thus there is considerable pressure on the patient to accept the role of the mentally ill as part of his self-conception.

28. W. Caudill, F. C. Redlich, H. R. Gilmore, and E. B. Brody, "Social Structure and Interaction Processes on a Psychiatric Ward," *American Journal of Orthopsychiatry*, 22 (April, 1952), pp. 314-334.

7. *Labeled deviants are punished when they attempt the return to conventional roles.* The second process operative is the systematic blockage of entry to non-deviant roles once the label has been publicly applied.[29] Thus the former mental patient, although he is urged to rehabilitate himself in the community, usually finds himself discriminated against in seeking to return to his old status, and on trying to find a new one in the occupational, marital, social, and other spheres.

Recent studies have shown that former mental patients, like ex-convicts, may find it difficult to find employment, even when their behavior and qualifications are unexceptionable. In an experimental study, Phillips has shown that the rejection of the mentally ill is largely a matter of stigmatization, rather than an evaluation of their behavior:

Despite the fact that the "normal" person is more an "ideal type" than a normal person, when he is described as having been in a mental hospital he is rejected more than psychotic individuals described as not seeking help or as seeing a clergyman, and more than a depressed-neurotic seeing a clergyman. Even when the normal person is described as (only) seeing a psychiatrist, he is rejected more than a simple schizophrenic who seeks no help, (and) more than a phobic-compulsive individual seeking no help or seeing a clergyman or physician.[30]

Propositions 6 and 7, taken together, suggest that to a degree the labeled deviant is rewarded for deviating, and punished for attempting to conform.

29. Lemert, *op. cit.*, provides an extensive discussion of this process under the heading of "Limitation of Participation," pp. 434-440.

30. D. L. Phillips, "Rejection: A Possible Consequence of Seeking Help for Mental Disorder," *American Sociological Review*, 28 (December, 1963), pp. 963-973.

8. *In the crisis occurring when a residual rule-breaker is publicly labeled, the deviant is highly suggestible, and may accept the proffered role of the insane as the only alternative.* When gross rule-breaking is publicly recognized and made an issue, the rule-breaker may be profoundly confused, anxious, and ashamed. In this crisis it seems reasonable to assume that the rule-breaker will be suggestible to the cues that he gets from the reactions of others toward him.[31] But those around him are also in a crisis; the incomprehensible nature of the rule-breaking, and the seeming need for immediate action lead them to take collective action against the rule-breaker on the basis of the attitude which all share—the traditional stereotypes of insanity. The rule-breaker is sensitive to the cues provided by these others and begins to think of himself in terms of the stereotyped role of insanity, which is part of his own role vocabulary also, since he, like those reacting to him, learned it early in childhood. In this situation his behavior may begin to follow the pattern suggested by his own stereotypes and the reactions of others. That is, when a residual rule-breaker organizes his behavior within the framework of mental disorder, and when his organization is validated by others, particularly prestigeful others such as physicians, he is "hooked" and will proceed on a career of chronic deviance.

There is little direct evidence for the part played by role images in the development of mental illness, but there are various suggestions that it may be an important one. For example, Rogler and Hollingshead, in their study of schizophrenia in Puerto Rico, give considerable emphasis to the role of the *loco* (lunatic) in the cases

31. This proposition receives support from K. T. Erikson's observations (*loc. cit*).

they studied. Comparing the forty persons diagnosed as schizophrenic with the control group, they state:

The role of the *loco* presents a problem to nearly all schizophrenic persons but to only a few who are free of the illness. Sick persons are extraordinarily defensive about the topic of the loco. Time and again, they state that they are not *locos* when no such question is being asked. When asked directly, only one sick person states that he is a *loco*; only one spouse of a sick person asserts this of his mate. The remaining persons in the sick group do not admit to *locura*. Rather, after a forceful denial, they add such phrases as: "Sometimes I act like one, but I am not one." "I may eventually become one, but I am not one now." "If I don't get help, I may become *loco*." "Perhaps I am on the road to becoming one." "Only at times do I act like a *loco*.[32]

Although all but two of the forty persons diagnosed as schizophrenic denied being *loco* in response to direct questions, the fact that they themselves raised the issue when the question was not asked suggests that the role image of the *loco* was being used in their own thought processes, regardless of their explicit denial. It is important for the reader to understand that the diagnosis of schizophrenia was made as part of the research process in this study, and not necessarily officially in the community. The subjects were persons who had sought psychiatric help, and who were diagnosed as schizophrenic by a psychiatrist attached to the research group. From the point of view presented here, we may consider the "sick" (i.e., schizophrenic) group as persons who are experimenting with the role of the mentally ill.

Rogler and Hollingshead also found that the role

32. L. H. Rogler and A. B. Hollingshead, *Trapped: Families and Schizophrenia* (New York: Wiley, 1965), p. 221.

image of the *loco* held by the "sick" group was not different from that held by the rest of the community.

Schizophrenic persons are particularly vulnerable to being assigned the role of the *loco*. Consequently, we explored the possibility that the schizophrenic's portrayal of this role would be drawn in less harsh and more benign terms than that drawn by well people. This idea was erroneous! There is no tendency on the part of the schizophrenics to soften the portrait of the *loco*; sick and well persons describe him as violent, immoral, criminal, filthy, idiosyncratic, and worthless. Moreover, men and women do not differ in their conceptions of the *loco*. Their views are uniform and deep; perhaps they are fixed unalterably.[33]

This finding is in accord with Propositions 4 and 5: if deviant role imagery is learned early and continually reaffirmed, a person's image of insanity would not be likely to be affected even when he himself runs the risk of being labeled. The role images are integral parts of the social structure and therefore not easily relinquished. Holding these relatively fixed images, the rule-breaker, like those around him, is susceptible to social suggestion in a crisis.

The role of suggestion is noted by Warner in his description of bone-pointing magic:

The effect of (the suggestion of the entire community on the victim) is obviously drastic. An analogous situation in our society is hard to imagine. If all a man's near kin, his father, mother, brothers and sisters, wife, children, business associates, friends, and all the other members of the society, should suddenly withdraw themselves because of some dramatic circumstance, refusing to take any attitude but one of taboo . . . and then perform over him a sacred ceremony . . . the enormous suggestive power of this movement . . . of the community after it has had its attitudes

33. *Ibid.*, p. 218.

(toward the victim) crystallized can be somewhat understood by ourselves.[34]

If we substitute for black magic the taboo that usually accompanies mental disorder, and consider a commitment proceeding or even mental hospital admission as a sacred ceremony, the similarity between Warner's description and the typical events in the development of mental disorder is considerable.

The last three propositions suggest that once a person has been placed in a deviant status there are rewards for conforming to the deviant role, and punishments for not conforming to the deviant role. This is not to imply, however, that the symptomatic behavior of persons occupying a deviant status is always a manifestation of conforming behavior. To explain this point, some discussion of the process of self-control in "normals" is necessary.

In a recent discussion of the process of self-control, Shibutani notes that self-control is not automatic, but is an intricate and delicately balanced process, sustainable only under propitious circumstances.[35] He points out that fatigue, the reaction to narcotics, excessive excitement or tension (such as is generated in mobs), or a number of other conditions interfere with self-control; conversely, conditions which produce normal bodily states, and deliberative processes such as symbolization and imaginative rehearsal before action, facilitate it.

One might argue that a crucially important aspect of imaginative rehearsal is the image of himself that the actor projects into his future action. Certainly in American society, the cultural image of the "normal" adult is

34. W. L. Warner, *A Black Civilization* (New York: Harper, 1958), rev. ed., p. 242.

35. T. Shibutani, *Society and Personality* (Englewood Cliffs, N.J.: Prentice-Hall, 1961), Chapter 6, "Consciousness and Voluntary Conduct."

that of a person endowed with self-control ("will power," "backbone," or "strength of character"). For the person who sees himself as endowed with the trait of self-control, self-control is facilitated, since he can imagine himself enduring stress during his imaginative rehearsal, and also while under actual stress.

For a person who has acquired an image of himself as lacking the ability to control his own actions, the process of self-control is likely to break down under stress. Such a person may feel that he has reached his "breaking-point" under circumstances which would be endured by a person with a "normal" self-conception. This is to say, a greater lack of self-control than can be explained by stress tends to appear in those roles for which the culture transmits imagery which emphasizes lack of self-control. In American society such imagery is transmitted for the roles of the very young and very old, drunkards and drug addicts, gamblers, and the mentally ill.

Thus, the social role of the mentally ill has a different significance at different phases of residual deviance. When labeling first occurs, it merely gives a name to rule-breaking which has other roots. When (and if) the rule-breaking becomes an issue, and is not ignored or rationalized away, labeling may create a social type, a pattern of "symptomatic" behavior in conformity with the stereotyped expectations of others. Finally, to the extent that the deviant role becomes a part of the deviant's self-conception, his ability to control his own behavior may be impaired under stress, resulting in episodes of compulsive behavior.

The preceding eight hypotheses form the basis for the final causal hypothesis.

9. *Among residual rule-breakers, labeling is the single*

most important cause of careers of residual deviance. This hypothesis assumes that most residual rule-breaking, if it does not become the basis for entry into the sick role, will not lead to a deviant career.[36] The most usual case, according to the argument that has been advanced here, is that there will be few if any social consequences of residual rule-breaking. Occasionally, however, such rule-breaking may become the basis for major changes in the rule-breaker's social status, other than demotion to the status of a mental patient. The three excerpts which follow illustrate such shifts.

Case #1: Some of the Indian tribes of California accorded prestige principally to those who passed through certain trance experiences. Not all of these tribes believed that it was exclusively women who were so blessed, but among the Shasta this was the convention. Their shamans were women, and they were accorded the greatest prestige in the community. They were chosen because of their constitutional liability to trance and allied manifestations. One day the woman who was so destined, while she was about her usual work, fell suddenly to the ground. She had heard a voice speaking to her in tones of the greatest intensity. Turning, she had seen a man with drawn bow and arrow. He commanded her to sing on pain of being shot through the heart by his arrow, but under the stress of the experience she fell senseless. Her family gathered. She was lying rigidly, hardly breathing. They knew that for some time she had had dreams of a special character which

36. Sociologically, an occupational career can be defined as "the sequence of movements from one position to another in an occupational system made by any individual who works in that system" (H. S. Becker, *Outsiders,* [New York: Free Press, 1963] p. 24). Similarly, a deviant career is the sequence of movements from one stigmatized position to another in the sector of the larger social system that functions to maintain social control. For example, the frequently cited progression of young men from probation through detention centers and reform schools to prison, with intervening times spent out of prison, might be considered as recurring deviant career. For Becker's discussion of deviant careers, see *op. cit.*, pp. 25-39.

indicated a shamanistic calling, dreams of escaping grizzly bears, falling off cliffs or trees, or of being surrounded by swarms of yellow-jackets. The community knew therefore what to expect. After a few hours the woman began to moan gently and to roll about upon the ground, trembling violently. She was supposed to be repeating the song which she had been told to sing and which during the trance had been taught her by the spirit. As she revived, her moaning became more and more clearly the spirit's song until at last she called out the name of the spirit itself, and immediately blood oozed from her mouth.

When the woman had come to herself after the first encounter with her spirit, she danced that night her first initiatory shaman's dance. For three nights she danced, holding herself by a rope that was swung from the ceiling. On the third night she had to receive in her body her power from the spirit. She was dancing, and as she felt the approach of the moment she called out, "He will shoot me, he will shoot me." Her friends stood close, for when she reeled in a kind of cataleptic seizure, they had to seize her before she fell or she would die. . . . From this time on she continued to validate her supernatural power by further cataleptic demonstrations, and she was called upon in great emergencies of life and death, for curing and for divination and for counsel. She became in other words, by this procedure a woman of great power and importance.[37]

Case #2: [Samuel lived in the house of Eli, the priest. One night, as Samuel lay down, he heard a voice call his name] . . . and he answered, "Here am I." And he ran to Eli, and said, "Here am I; for thou callest me." And he said, "I called not; lie down again." And he went and lay down.

[Again Samuel heard his name called.] and Samuel arose and went to Eli, and said, "Here am I; for thou didst call me." And he answered, "I called not, my son; lie down again." [For the third

37. R. Benedict, *Patterns of Culture* (New York: Mentor, 1946), pp. 245-247.

time, Samuel heard his name called.] And he arose and went to Eli, and said, "Here am I, for thou didst call me." And Eli perceived that the Lord had called the child.

Therefore Eli said unto Samuel, "Go, lie down: and it shall be, if He call thee, that you shall say, Speak, Lord; for Thy servant heareth." So Samuel went and lay down in his place.

And the Lord came, and stood, and called as at other times, "Samuel, Samuel." Then Samuel answered, "Speak, Lord, for Thy servant heareth." [Samuel hears prophesied the downfall of the house of Eli.] And all Israel from Dan even to Beersheba knew that Samuel was established to be a prophet of the Lord.[38]

Case #3: Interviewer: "How did you first come to believe that you had psychic powers?"

Mrs. Bendit: ". . . during this particular period of my life, I was facing a number of personal problems that seemed overwhelming to me at the time. I was thoroughly depressed and confused, and I felt that the strain was getting progressively worse. I had been in this state for about two weeks, when one Sunday morning, in church, I was shocked to see, up in the rafters of the ceiling of the church, a group of angels. I couldn't keep my eyes from the sight, although I noticed that no one else in the congregation was look-ing up. After this experience, I wandered around for several days, hardly knowing what to do with myself. One evening soon after, I went to a reception, hoping to take my mind from my troubles.

"I stayed pretty much to myself at the party, but I soon noticed, that across the room there was a woman who was watching me intently. She finally came over to me and introduced herself. She then said, 'You are psychic, aren't you?'

"I asked her what she meant. She then explained clairvoyance to me at some length. I told her about my vision in the church. She explained that this experience was an example of my psychic powers. She said that she was a psychic, and that she could tell that I had the gift also. Although her explanation sounded strange

38. I Samuel 3.

to me, I felt somewhat relieved. In the ensuing weeks, I saw her often and we had lengthy conversations. She introduced me into the group of clairvoyants and interested persons that she belonged to . . . It was to this group that I first began to demonstrate my clairvoyance . . . Several years after this I was able to arrange, with the help of my husband (her husband is a physician) an appearance before the Royal Academy of Medicine, for a demonstration of clairvoyance."[39]

Cases 1 and 2 illustrate elevations in social status that are based on primary rule-breaking. Case 3 illustrates what might be called a lateral movement in status, since Mrs. Bendit has obviously become completely identified with her role as a clairvoyant.

The likelihood that residual rule-breaking in itself will not lead to labeling as a deviant draws attention to the central significance of the contingencies which influence the direction and intensity of the societal reaction. One of the urgent conceptual tasks for a sociological theory of deviant behavior is the development of a precise and widely applicable set of such contingencies. The classification that is offered here is only a crude first step in this direction.

Although there are a wide variety of contingencies which lead to labeling they can be simply classified in terms of the nature of the rule-breaking, the person who breaks the rules, and the community in which the rule-breaking occurs. Other things being equal, the severity of the societal reaction is a function of, first, the degree, amount and visibility of the rule-breaking; second, the power of the rule-breaker and the social distance between him and the agents of social control; and finally, the tolerance level of the community, and the availability

39. Interview on radio station KPFA, Berkeley, California, as recollected by the author.

in the culture of the community of alternative nondeviant roles.[40] Particularly crucial for future research is the importance of the first two contingencies (the amount and degree of rule-breaking), which are characteristics of the rule-breaker, relative to the remaining five contingencies, which are characteristics of the social system.[41] To the extent that these five factors are found empirically to be independent determinants of labeling and denial, the status of the mental patient can be considered a partly ascribed rather than a completely achieved status. The dynamics of treated mental illness could then be profitably studied quite apart from the individual dynamics of mental disorder, by focusing on social systemic contingencies.

A NOTE ON FEEDBACK IN DEVIANCE-AMPLIFYING SYSTEMS

It should be noted, however, that these contingencies are causal only because they become part of a dynamic system: the reciprocal and cumulative inter-relation between the rule-breaker's behavior and the societal reaction.[42] For example, the more the rule-breaker enters the role of the mentally ill, the more he is defined by others as mentally ill; but the more he is defined as mentally ill,

40. *Cf.* Lemert, *op. cit.*, pp. 51-53, 55-68; Goffman, "The Moral Career of the Mental Patient," in *Asylums, op. cit.*, p. 134-135; D. Mechanic, "Some Factors in Identifying and Defining Mental Illness," *Mental Hygiene*, 46 (January, 1962), pp. 66-74. For a list of similar factors in the reaction to physical illness, see E. L. Koos, *The Health of Regionville* (New York: Columbia University Press, 1954), pp. 30-38.

41. *Cf.* S. Dinitz, M. Lefton, S. Angrist, and B. Pasamanick, "Psychiatric and Social Attributes as Predictors of Case Outcome in Mental Hospitalization," *Social Problems*, 8 (Spring, 1961), pp. 322-328; and Study II in Chapter 5.

42. For an explicit treatment of feedback, see E. M. Lemert, "Paranoia and the Dynamics of Exclusion," *Sociometry*, 25 (March, 1962), pp. 2-20.

the more fully he enters the role, and so on. This kind of vicious circle is quite characteristic of many different kinds of social and individual systems. It is very important to understand the part that social contingencies play in such a system, since the cause-effect relationship is not a simple one.

In the Rogler and Hollingshead study of schizophrenia in Puerto Rico, (referred to above) the authors drew attention to the dynamic interrelation between role entry and changes in the deviant's self-conception.

Although the sick person is deeply absorbed in his illness and yearns to speak about it, confidants are carefully selected. The illness is suppressed as a topic of conversation with friends and associates. Efforts are made to pretend that he is not a *loco*. He controls activities which exacerbate his *loco*-like behavior. These efforts are relatively futile, however, as the symptoms of the illness are strong and readily visible in the crowded social setting in which he lives. In point of fact, the sick person has begun to be viewed and treated as a *loco*. He withdraws from society out of fear that he will be stigmatized as a *loco*. In turn, the rejection by his friends and associates pushes him to withdraw. The stigma attached to this role is so strong that the withdrawal of the sick person from participation in all types of social groups appears to be a natural sequel to the condemnation he suffers.[43]

The process described in this passage can be interpreted as a vicious circle begun by stigmatization, withdrawal to avoid more stigma, stigmatization because of withdrawal or its effects, and so on around the circle.

The vicious circle effect occurs not only in the entrance to role-playing by the rule-breaker, but in other parts of the system also. In order to see this more clearly,

43. Rogler and Hollingshead, *op. cit.*, pp. 241-242.

it is useful to represent the theory as a flow chart, as in Chart 1.[44]

This chart makes it clear that the theory of stable mental disorder discussed here is actually an assembly of system modules, which interact. There is the module of residual rule-breaking, the contingency module which filters out most of the rule-breakers through denial, the crisis module, the rule-breaker's self-conception module, the social control module, which operates such that the deviant tends to play the stereotyped deviant role, and finally, the compulsive behavior module. Each of these modules is a system in itself, with its own contingencies. In the context of the larger theory, however, each is a sub-system, which, under proper conditions, operates as part of the entire network.

The total system forms what Maruyama has called a "deviation-amplifying system," in which low probability events are stabilized. In such a system, the simple causal laws in which similar conditions of deviance produce similar effects is not operative. Even more complicated models of contingent cause do not work, because it is necessary to specify the state of the entire system.

In cybernetic terms, what we have referred to as a vicious circle is called positive feedback, and it is apparent from the chart that there are a number of feedback loops in the system. The episodes of compulsive behavior interact with the earlier crisis, other's responses, and the deviant's self-conception sub-systems, and the playing of the deviant role feeds back to the system of social control and the deviant's self-conception as well. Under proper conditions, deviation is not damped out by the

44. W. Buckley suggested the use of this flow chart, and provided help in interpreting the theory in cybernetic terms. For comment by Buckley, see his "Methodological Note" in the Appendix.

CHART NO. 1 FLOW CHART—STABILIZATION OF DEVIANCE IN A SOCIAL SYSTEM

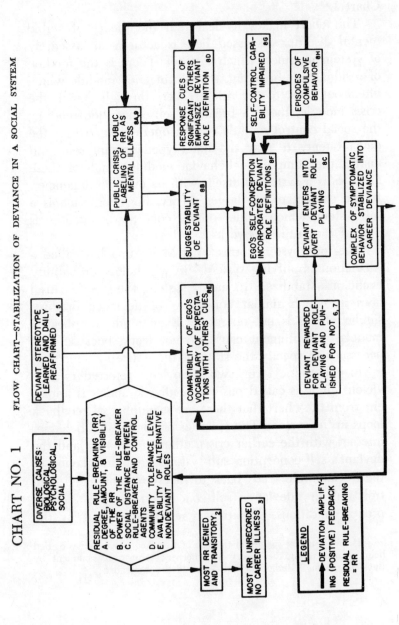

DIVERSE CAUSES: BIOLOGICAL, PSYCHOLOGICAL, SOCIAL 1

RESIDUAL RULE-BREAKING (RR)
A. DEGREE, AMOUNT, & VISIBILITY OF THE RR
B. POWER OF THE RULE-BREAKER
C. SOCIAL DISTANCE BETWEEN RULE-BREAKER AND CONTROL AGENTS
D. COMMUNITY TOLERANCE LEVEL
E. AVAILABILITY OF ALTERNATIVE NONDEVIANT ROLES

MOST RR DENIED AND TRANSITORY 2

MOST RR UNRECORDED NO CAREER ILLNESS 3

DEVIANT STEREOTYPE LEARNED AND DAILY REAFFIRMED 4, 5

PUBLIC CRISIS, PUBLIC LABELING OF RR AS MENTAL ILLNESS 8A

RESPONSE CUES OF SIGNIFICANT OTHERS EMPHASIZE DEVIANT ROLE DEFINITION 8D

SELF-CONTROL CAPABILITY IMPAIRED 8G

EPISODES OF COMPULSIVE BEHAVIOR 8H

SUGGESTABILITY OF DEVIANT 8B

COMPATIBILITY OF EGO'S VOCABULARY OF EXPECTATIONS WITH OTHERS' CUES 8E

EGO'S SELF-CONCEPTION INCORPORATES DEVIANT ROLE DEFINITIONS 8F

DEVIANT ENTERS INTO OVERT DEVIANT ROLE-PLAYING 8C

DEVIANT REWARDED FOR DEVIANT ROLE-PLAYING AND PUNISHED FOR NOT 6, 7

COMPLEX OF SYMPTOMATIC BEHAVIOR STABILIZED INTO CAREER DEVIANCE

BACK TO COMMUNITY

LEGEND
→ DEVIATION AMPLIFYING (POSITIVE) FEEDBACK
RESIDUAL RULE-BREAKING = RR

action of the system, which is the usual situation in social systems, but is stabilized or even amplified.

CONCLUSION

The discussion to this point has presented a sociological theory of the causation of stable mental disorder. Since the evidence advanced in support of the theory was scattered and fragmentary, it can only be suggested as a stimulus to further discussion and research. Among the areas pointed out for further investigation are field studies of the prevalence and duration of residual rule-breaking; investigations of stereotypes of mental disorder in children, the mass media, and adult conversations; studies of the rewarding of stereotyped deviation, blockage of return to conventional roles, and of the suggestibility of rule-breakers in crises. The final causal hypothesis suggests studies of the conditions under which denial and labeling of residual rule-breaking occur. The variable which might effect the societal reaction concern the nature of the rule-breaking, the rule-breaker himself, and the community in which the rule-breaking occurs. Although many of the hypotheses suggested are largely unverified, they suggest avenues for investigating mental disorder different than those that are usually followed, and the rudiments of a general theory of deviant behavior. In Chapter 5 a study of hospitalization and release based upon this theory will be described.

PART
II

Research

PART TWO

II

Research

4

Decisions in Medicine

THE discussion to this point has concerned a theory of stable mental illness. In this chapter[1] and the following chapter, our attention shifts from theory to practice. In Chapter 5, two studies of psychiatric decision-making are reported which are relevant to our theoretical concerns. This chapter introduces the studies in Chapter 5 by a discussion of a decision-making problem that psychiatry shares with general medicine. Members of professions such as law and medicine frequently are confronted with uncertainty in the course of their routine duties. In these circumstances, informal norms have developed for handling uncertainty so that paralyzing hesitation is avoided. These norms are based upon assumptions that some types of error are more to be avoided than others— assumptions so basic that they are usually taken for granted, are seldom discussed, and are therefore slow to change.

The purpose of this chapter is to describe one important norm for handling uncertainty in medical diagnosis, that judging a sick person well is more to be avoided than judging a well person sick, and to suggest

1. An earlier version of this chapter was presented as a paper at the Conference on Mathematical Models in the Behavioral and Social Sciences, sponsored by the Western Management Science Institute, University of California at Los Angeles, Cambria, California, 1961.

some of the consequences of the application of this norm in medical practice. Apparently this norm, like many important cultural norms, "goes without saying" in the subculture of the medical profession; in form, however, it resembles any decision rule for guiding behavior under conditions of uncertainty. In the discussion that follows, decision rules in law, statistics, and medicine are compared, in order to indicate the types of error that are thought to be the more important to avoid and the assumptions underlying this preference. On the basis of recent findings of the widespread distribution of elements of disease and deviance in normal populations, the assumption of a uniform relationship between disease signs and impairment is criticized. Finally, it is suggested that to the extent that physicians are guided by this medical decision rule, they too often place patients in the "sick role" who could otherwise have continued in their normal pursuits.

To the extent that physicians and the public are biased toward treatment, the "creation" of illness, i.e., the production of unnecessary impairment, may go hand in hand with the prevention and treatment of disease in modern medicine. The magnitude of the bias toward treatment in any single case may be quite small, since there are probably other medical decision rules ("When in doubt, delay your decision") which counteract the rule discussed here. Even a small bias, however, if it is relatively constant throughout Western society, can have effects of large magnitude. Since this argument is based largely on fragmentary evidence, it is intended merely to stimulate further discussion and research, rather than to demonstrate the validity of a point of view. The discussion will begin with the consideration of a decision rule in law.

In criminal trials in England and the United States, there is an explicit rule for arriving at decisions in the face of uncertainty: "A man is innocent until proven guilty." The meaning of this rule is made clear by the English common-law definition of the phrase "proven guilty," which according to tradition is that the judge or jury must find the evidence of guilt compelling *beyond a reasonable doubt*. The basic legal rule for arriving at a decision in the face of uncertainty may be briefly stated: "When in doubt, acquit." That is, the jury or judge must not be equally wary of erroneously convicting or acquitting: the error that is most important to avoid is to erroneously convict. This concept is expressed in the maxim, "Better a thousand guilty men go free, than one innocent man be convicted."

The reasons underlying this rule seem clear. It is assumed that in most cases, a conviction will do irreversible harm to an individual by damaging his reputation in the eyes of his fellows. The individual is seen as weak and defenseless, relative to society, and therefore in no position to sustain the consequences of an erroneous decision. An erroneous acquittal, on the other hand, damages society. If an individual who has actually committed a crime is not punished, he may commit the crime again, or more important, the deterrent effect of punishment for the violation of this crime may be diminished for others. Although these are serious outcomes they are generally thought not to be as serious as the consequences of erroneous conviction for the innocent individual, since society is able to sustain an indefinite number of such errors without serious consequences. For these and perhaps other reasons, the decision rule to assume innocence exerts a powerful influence on legal proceedings.

TYPE 1 AND TYPE 2 ERRORS

Deciding on guilt or innocence is a special case of a problem to which statisticians have given considerable attention, the testing of hypotheses. Since most scientific work is done with samples, statisticians have developed techniques to guard against results which are due to chance sampling fluctuations. The problem, however, is that one might reject a finding that was actually correct as due to sampling fluctuations. There are, therefore, two kinds of errors: rejecting a hypothesis that is true, and accepting one that is false. Usually the hypothesis is stated so that the former error (rejecting a hypothesis which is true) is the error that is thought to be the more important to avoid. This type of error is called an "error of the first kind," or a Type 1 error. The latter error (accepting a hypothesis which is false) is the less important error to avoid, and is called an "error of the second kind," or a Type 2 error.[2]

To guard against chance fluctuations in sampling, statisticians test the probability that findings could have arisen by chance. At some predetermined probability (called the alpha level), usually 0.05 or less, the possibility that the findings arose by chance is rejected. This level means that there are five chances in a hundred that one will reject a hypothesis which is true. Although these five chances indicate a real risk of error, it is not common to set the level much lower (say 0.001) because this raises the probability of making an error of the second kind.

A similar dilemma faces the judge or jury in deciding

2. J. Neyman, *First Course in Probability and Statistics* (New York: Holt, 1950), pp. 265-266.

whether to convict or acquit in the face of uncertainty. Particularly in the adversary system of law, where professional attorneys seek to advance their arguments and refute those of their opponents, there is often considerable uncertainty even as to the facts of the case, let alone intangibles like intent. The maxim, "Better a thousand guilty men should go free, than one innocent man be convicted," would mean, if taken literally rather than as a rhetorical flourish, that the alpha level for legal decisions is set quite low.

Although the legal decision rule is not expressed in as precise a form as a statistical decision rule, it represents a very similar procedure for dealing with uncertainty. There is one respect, however, in which it is quite different. Statistical decision procedures are recognized by those who use them as mere conveniences, which can be varied according to the circumstances. The legal decision rule, in contrast, is an inflexible and binding moral rule, which carries with it the force of long sanction and tradition. The assumption of innocence is a part of the social institution of law in Western society; it is explicitly stated in legal codes, and is accepted as legitimate by jurists and usually by the general populace, with only occasional grumbling, e.g., a criminal is seen as "getting off" because of "legal technicalities."

DECISION RULES IN MEDICINE

Although the analogous rule for decisions in medicine is not as explicitly stated as the rule in law and probably is considerably less rigid, it would seem that there is such a rule in medicine which is as imperative in its operation as its analogue in law. Do physicians and the general public consider that rejecting the hypothesis of

illness when it is true, or accepting it when it is false, is
the error that is most important to avoid? It seems fairly
clear that the rule in medicine may be stated as: "When
in doubt, continue to suspect illness." That is, for a physician to dismiss a patient when he is actually ill is a
Type 1 error, and to retain a patient when he is not ill
is a Type 2 error.

Most physicians learn early in their training that it
is far more culpable to dismiss a sick patient than to retain a well one. This rule is so pervasive and fundamental
that it goes unstated in textbooks on diagnosis. It is occasionally mentioned explicitly in other contexts, however. Neyman, for example, in his discussion of X-ray
screening for tuberculosis states:

[If the patient is actually well, but the hypothesis that he is sick
is accepted, a Type 2 error] then the patient will suffer some un-
justified anxiety and, perhaps, will be put to some unnecessary
expense until further studies of his health will establish that any
alarm about the state of his chest is unfounded. Also, the unjusti-
fied precautions ordered by the clinic may somewhat affect its
reputation. On the other hand, should the hypothesis [of sickness]
be true and yet the accepted hypothesis be [that he is well, a
Type 1 error], then the patient will be in danger of losing the
precious opportunity of treating the incipient disease in its beginning stages when the cure is not so difficult. Furthermore, the
oversight by the clinic's specialist of the dangerous condition would
affect the clinic's reputation even more than the unnecessary alarm.
From this point of view, it appears that the error of rejecting the
hypothesis [of sickness] when it is true is *far more important* to
avoid than the error of accepting the hypothesis (of illness) when
it is false.[3] [Italics added]

Although this particular discussion pertains to tuber-

3. *Ibid.*, p. 270.

culosis, it is pertinent to many other diseases also. From casual conversations with physicians, the impression one gains is that this moral lesson is deeply ingrained in the physician's personal code.

It is not only physicians who feel this way, however. This rule is grounded both in legal proceedings and in popular sentiment. Although there is some sentiment against Type 2 errors (unnecessary surgery, for instance), it has nothing like the force and urgency of the sentiment against Type 1 errors. A physician who dismisses a patient who subsequently dies of a disease that should have been detected is not only subject to legal action for negligence and possible loss of license for incompetence, but also to moral condemnation from his colleagues and from his own conscience for his delinquency. Nothing remotely resembling this amount of moral and legal suasion is brought to bear for committing a Type 2 error. Indeed, this error is sometimes seen as sound clinical practice, indicating a healthily conservative approach to medicine.

The discussion to this point suggests that physicians follow a decision rule which may be stated, "When in doubt, diagnose illness." If physicians are actually influenced by this rule, then studies of the validity of diagnosis should demonstrate the operation of the rule. That is, we should expect that objective studies of diagnostic errors should show that Type 1 and Type 2 errors do not occur with equal frequency, but in fact, that Type 2 errors far outnumber Type 1 errors. Unfortunately for our purposes, however, there are apparently only a few studies which provide the type of data which would adequately test the hypothesis. Although studies of the reliability of diagnosis abound[4] showing that physicians

4. L. H. Garland, "Studies on the Accuracy of Diagnostic Procedures," *American Journal of Roentgenology, Radium Therapy, and Nuclear Medicine,* 82 (1959), pp. 25-38.

disagree with each other in their diagnoses of the same patients, these studies do not report the validity of diagnosis, or the types of error which are made, with the following exceptions.

We can infer that Type 2 errors outnumber Type 1 errors from Bakwin's study of physicians' judgments regarding the advisability of tonsillectomy for 1,000 school children. "Of these, some 611 had had their tonsils removed. The remaining 389 were then examined by other physicians, and 174 were selected for tonsillectomy. This left 215 children whose tonsils were apparently normal. Another group of doctors was put to work examining these 215 children, and 99 of them were adjudged in need of tonsillectomy. Still another group of doctors was then employed to examine the remaining children, and nearly one-half were recommended for operation."[5] Almost half of each group of children were judged to be in need of the operation. Even assuming that a small proportion of children needing tonsillectomy were missed in each examination (Type 1 error), the number of Type 2 errors in this study far exceeded the number of Type 1 errors.

In the field of roentgenology, studies of diagnostic error are apparently more highly developed than in other areas of medicine. Garland summarizes these findings, reporting that in a study of 14,867 films for tuberculosis signs, there were 1,216 positive readings which turned out to be clinically negative (Type 2 error) and only 24 negative readings which turned out to be clinically active (Type 1 error)![6] This ratio (about 50 to 1) is apparently a fairly typical finding in roentgenographic studies. Since physicians are well aware of the provi-

5. H. Bakwin, "Pseudocia Pediatricia," *New England Journal of Medicine*, 232 (1945), pp. 691-697.
6. Garland, *op. cit.*, p. 31.

sional nature of radiological findings, this great discrepancy between the frequency of the types of error in film screening is not too alarming. On the other hand, it does provide objective evidence of the operation of the decision rule "Better safe than sorry."

BASIC ASSUMPTIONS

The logic of this decision rule rests on two assumptions:

1. Disease is usually a determinate, inevitably unfolding process, which, if undetected and untreated, will grow to a point where it endangers the life or limb of the individual, and in the case of contagious diseases, the lives of others. This is not to say, of course, that physicians think of all diseases as determinate: witness the concept of the "benign" condition. The point here is that the imagery of disease which the physician uses in attempting to reach a decision, his working hypothesis, is *usually* based on the deterministic model of disease.

2. Medical diagnosis of illness, unlike legal judgment, is not an irreversible act which does untold damage to the status and reputation of the patient. A physician may search for illness for an indefinitely long time, causing inconvenience for the patient, perhaps, but in the typical case doing the patient no irradicable harm. Obviously, again, physicians do not always make this assumption. A physician who suspects epilepsy in a truck driver knows full well that his patient will probably never drive a truck again if the diagnosis is made, and the physician will go to great lengths to avoid a Type 2 error in this situation. Similarly, if a physician suspects that a particular patient has hypochondriacal trends, the physician

will lean in the direction of a Type 1 error in a situation
of uncertainty. These and other similar situations are
exceptions, however. The physician's *usual* working assumption is that medical observation and diagnosis, in
itself, is neutral and innocuous, relative to the dangers
resulting from disease.[7]

In the light of these two assumptions, therefore, it
is seen as far better for the physician to chance a Type 2
error than a Type 1 error. These two assumptions will be
examined and criticized in the remainder of the paper.
The assumption that Type 2 errors are relatively harmless will be considered first.

In recent discussions it is increasingly recognized
that in one area of medicine, psychiatry, the assumption
that medical diagnosis can cause no irreversible harm to
the patient's status is dubious. Psychiatric treatment, in
many segments of the population and for many occupations, raises a question about the person's social status.
It could be argued that in making a medical diagnosis
the psychiatrist comes very close to making a legal decision, with its ensuing consequences for the person's
reputation. One might argue that the Type 2 error in
psychiatry, of judging a well person, is at least as much
to be avoided as the Type 1 error, of judging the sick
person well. Yet the psychiatrist's moral orientation, since
he is first and foremost a physician, is guided by the
medical, rather than the legal, decision rule. The psychiatrist continues to be more willing to err on the conservative side, to diagnose as ill when the person is healthy,

7. Even though this assumption is widely held, it has been vigor-
ously criticized within the medical profession. See, for example, W.
Darley, "What is the Next Step in Preventive Medicine?", *Association
of Teachers Preventive Medicine Newsletter*, 1959, p. 6. For a witty
criticism of both assumptions, see H. Ratner, "Medicine," *Interviews
on the American Character* (Santa Barbara, California: Center for the
Study of Democratic Institutions, 1962).

even though it is no longer clear that this error is any more desirable than its opposite.

There is a more fundamental question about this decision rule, however, which concerns both physical illness and mental disorder. This question primarily concerns the first assumption, that disease is a determinate process. It also implicates the second assumption, that medical treatment does not have irreversible effects.

In recent years physicians and social scientists have reported finding disease signs and deviant behavior prevalent in normal, non-institutionalized populations. It has been shown, for instance, that deviant acts, some of a serious nature, are widely admitted by persons in random samples of normal populations.[8] There is some evidence which suggests that grossly deviant, "psychotic" behavior has at least temporarily existed in relatively large proportions of a normal population.[9] Finally, there is a growing body of evidence that many signs of physical disease are distributed quite widely in normal populations. A recent survey of simple high blood pressure indicated that the prevalence ranged from 11.4 to 37.2 per cent in the various subgroups studied.[10]

8. J. S. Wallerstein, and C. J. Wyle, "Our Law—Abiding Law-Breakers," *Probation*, 25 (1947), pp. 107-112; A. L. Porterfield, *Youth in Trouble* (Fort Worth, Texas; Lee Potishman Foundation, 1946); A. C. Kinsey, W. B. Pomeroy, and C. E. Martin, *Sexual Behavior in the Human Male* (Philadelphia and London: W. B. Saunders, 1948).

9. R. J. Plunkett, and J. E. Gordon, *Epidemiology and Mental Illness* (New York: Basic Books, 1961); J. A. Clausen and M. R. Yarrow, "Paths to the Mental Hospital," *Journal of Social Issues*, 11 (1955), pp. 25-32.

10. P. M. Rautaharju, M. J. Korvonen, and A. Keys, "The Frequency of Arteriosclerotic and Hypertensive Heart Disease in Ostensibly Healthy Working Populations in Finland," *Journal of Chronic Diseases*, 13 (1961), pp. 426-438. *Cf.* J. Stokes, and T. R. Dawber, "The 'Silent Coronary': the Frequency and Clinical Characteristics of Unrecognized Myocardial Infarction in the Framingham Study," *Annals of Internal Medicine*, 50 (1959) pp. 1359-1369; J. P. Dunn and L. E. Etter, "Inadequacy of the Medical History in the Diagnosis of Duodenal Ulcer," *New England Journal of Medicine*, 266 (1962), pp. 68-72.

As stated in Chapter II, physical defects and "psychiatric" deviancy exist in an uncrystallized form in large segments of the population. Lemert calls this type of behavior, which is often transitory, *primary deviation*.[11] In his discussion of the doctor-patient relationship, Balint speaks of similar behavior as the "unorganized phase of illness."[12] Balint seems to take for granted, however, that patients will eventually "settle down" to an "organized" illness. Yet it is possible that other outcomes may occur. A person in this stage might change jobs or wives instead, or merely continue in the primary deviation state indefinitely, without getting better or worse.

This discussion suggests that in order to estimate the probability that a person with a disease sign would become incapacitated because of the development of disease, investigations quite unlike existing studies would need to be conducted. These would be longitudinal studies in a random sample of a normal population, of outcomes in persons having signs of diseases in which no attempt was made to arrest the disease. It is true that there are a number of longitudinal studies in which the effects of treatment are compared with the effects of nontreatment. These studies, however, have always been conducted with clinical groups, rather than with persons with disease signs who were located in field studies.[13] Even clinical trials appear to offer many difficulties, both

11. E. M. Lemert, *Social Pathology* (New York: McGraw-Hill, 1951).

12. M. Balint, *The Doctor, His Patient, and the Illness* (New York: International Universities Press, 1957).

13. The Framingham Study is an exception to this statement. Even in this study, however, experimental procedures (random assignment to treatment and non-treatment groups) were not used. T. R. Dawber, F. E. Moore and G. V. Mann, "Coronary Heart Disease in the Framingham Study," *American Journal of Public Health* 47 (April 1957), Part 2, pp. 4-24.

from the ethical and scientific points of view.[14] These difficulties would be increased many times in controlled field trials, as would the problems which concern the amount of time and money necessary. Without such studies, nevertheless, the meaning of many common disease signs remains somewhat equivocal.

Given the relatively small amount of knowledge about the distributions and natural outcomes of many diseases, it is possible that our conceptions of the danger of disease are exaggerated. To mention again the dramatic example cited earlier, until the late 1940's, histoplasmosis was thought to be a rare tropical disease, with a uniform fatal outcome. Recently, however, it was discovered that it is widely prevalent, and with fatal outcome or impairment extremely rare.[15] It is conceivable that other diseases, such as some types of heart disease and mental disorder, may prove to be similar in character. Although no actuarial studies have been made which would yield the true probabilities of impairment, physicians usually set the Type 1 level quite high, because they believe that the probability of impairment from making a Type 2 error is quite low. Let us now examine that assumption.

THE "SICK ROLE"

If, as has been argued here, much illness goes unattended without serious consequences, the assumption that medical diagnosis has no irreversible effects on the patient seems questionable.

The patient's attitude to his illness is usually considerably changed

14. A. B. Hill, *Controlled Clinical Trials* (Springfield, Ill.: Charles C Thomas, 1960).
15. J. Schwartz and G. L. Baum, "The History of Histoplasmosis," *New England Journal of Medicine*, 256 (1957), pp. 253-258.

during, and by, the series of physical examinations. These changes, which may profoundly influence the course of a chronic illness, are not taken seriously by the medical profession and, though occasionally mentioned, they have never been the subject of a proper scientific investigation.[16]

There are grounds for believing that persons who avail themselves of professional services are under considerable strain and tension (if the problem could have been easily solved, they would probably have used more informal means of handling it.) Social-psychological principles indicate that persons under strain are highly suggestible, particularly to suggestions from a prestigeful source, such as a physician.

It can be argued that the Type 2 error involves the danger of having a person enter the "sick role"[17] in circumstances where no serious result would ensue if the illness were unattended. Perhaps the combination of a physician determined to find disease *signs*, if they are to be found, and the suggestible patient, searching for subjective *symptoms* among the many amorphous and usually unattended bodily impulses, is often sufficient to unearth a disease which changes the patient's status from that of well to sick, and may also have effect on his familial and occupational status. (In Lemert's terms, the illness would be *secondary deviation* after the person has entered the sick role.)[18]

There is a considerable body of evidence in the medical literature concerning the process in which the physician unnecessarily causes the patient to enter the sick role. Thus, in a discussion of "iatrogenic" (physician-induced) heart disease, this point is made:

16. Balint, *op. cit.*, p. 43.
17. T. Parsons, "Illness and the Role of the Physician," *American Journal of Orthopsychiatry*, 21 (1950), pp. 452-460.
18. Lemert, *op. cit.*

The physician, by calling attention to a murmur or some cardio-vascular abnormality, even though functionally insignificant, may precipitate [symptoms of heart disease]. The experience of the work classification units of cardiac-in-industry programs, where patients with cardiovascular disease are evaluated as to work capacity, gives impressive evidence regarding the high incidence of such functional manifestations in persons with the diagnosis of cardiac lesion.[19]

Although there is a tendency in medicine to dismiss this process as due to quirks of particular patients, e.g., as malingering, hypochondriasis, or as "merely functional disease" (that is, functional for the patient), causation probably lies not in the patient, but in medical procedures. Most people, perhaps, if they actually have the disease signs and are told by an authority, the physician, that they are ill, will obligingly come up with appropriate symptoms. A case history will illustrate this process. Under the heading "It may be well to let sleeping dogs lie," a physician recounts the following case:

Here is a woman, aged 40 years, who is admitted with symptoms of congestive cardiac failure, valvular disease, mitral stenosis and auricular fibrillation. She tells us that she did not know that there was anything wrong with her heart and that she had had no symptoms up to 5 years ago when her chest was x-rayed in the course of a mass radiography examination for tuberculosis. She was not suspected and this was only done in the course of routine at the factory. Her lungs were pronounced clear but she was told that she had an enlarged heart and was advised to go to a hospital for investigation and treatment. From that time she began to suffer from symptoms—breathlessness on exertion—and has been in the hospital 4 or 5 times since. Now she is here with congestive heart

19. J. V. Warren and J. Wolter, "Symptoms and Diseases Induced by the Physician," *General Practitioner*, 9 (1954), pp. 77-84.

failure. She cannot understand why, from the time that her enlarged heart was discovered, she began to get symptoms.[20]

What makes this kind of "role-taking" extremely important is that it can occur even when the diagnostic label is kept from the patient. By the way he is handled, the patient can usually infer the nature of the diagnosis, since in his uncertainty and anxiety he is extremely sensitive to subtleties in the physician's behavior. An example of this process (already cited in Chapter 2) is found in reports on treatment of battle fatigue. Speaking of psychiatric patients in the Sicilian campaign during World War II, a psychiatrist notes:

Although patients were received at this hospital within 24 to 48 hours after their breakdown, a disappointing number, approximately 15 per cent, were salvaged for combat duty . . . any therapy, including usual interview methods that sought to uncover basic emotional conflicts or attempted to relate current behavior and symptoms with past personality patterns seemingly provided patients with logical reasons for their combat failure. The insights obtained by even such mild depth therapy readily convinced the patient and often his therapist that the limit of combat endurance had been reached as proved by vulnerable personality traits. Patients were obligingly cooperative in supplying details of their neurotic childhood, previous emotional difficulties, lack of aggressiveness and other dependency traits.[21]

Glass goes on to say that removal of the soldier from his unit for treatment of any kind usually resulted in long-term neurosis. In contrast, if the soldier was given

20. H. Gardiner-Hill, *Clinical Involvements* (London: Butterworth, 1958), p. 158.
21. A. J. Glass, "Psychotherapy in the Combat Zone," in *Symposium on Stress* (Washington, D.C.: Army Medical Service Graduate School, 1953).

only superficial psychiatric attention and *kept with his unit*, chronic impairment was usually avoided. The implication is that removal from the military unit and psychiatric treatment symbolizes to the soldier, behaviorally rather than with verbal labels, the "fact" that he is a mental case.

The traditional way of interpreting these reactions of the soldiers, and perhaps the civilian cases, is in terms of malingering or feigning illness. The process of taking roles, however, as it is conceived of here, is not completely or even largely voluntary. (For a sophisticated discussion of role-playing, see Goffman.[22]) Vaguely defined impulses become "real" to the participants when they are organized under any one of a number of more or less interchangeable social roles. It can be argued that when a person is in a confused and suggestible state, when he organizes his feelings and behavior by using the sick role, and when his choice of roles is validated by a physician or others, he is "hooked," and will proceed on a career of chronic illness.[23]

IMPLICATIONS FOR RESEARCH

The hypothesis suggested by the preceding discussion is that physicians and the public typically overvalue

22. E. Goffman, *The Presentation of Self in Everyday Life* (Garden City, N.Y.: Doubleday-Anchor, 1959), pp. 17-21.

23. Some of the findings of the Purdue Farm Cardiac Project support the position taken in this paper. It was found, for example, that "iatrogenics" took more health precautions than "hidden cardiacs," suggesting that entry into the sick role can cause more social incapacity than the actual disease does (R. L. Eichorn and R. M. Andersen, "Changes in Personal Adjustment to Perceived and Medically Established Heart Disease: A Panel Study," paper read at American Sociological Association Meeting, Washington, D.C., 1962).

medical treatment relative to non-treatment as a course of action in the face of uncertainty, and this overvaluation results in the creation as well as the prevention of impairment. This hypothesis, since it is based on scattered observations, is put forward only to point out several areas where systematic research is needed.

From the point of view of assessing the effectiveness of medical practice, this hypothesis is probably too general to be used directly. Needed for such a task are hypotheses concerning the conditions under which error is likely to occur, the type of error that is likely, and the consequences of each type of error. Significant dimensions of the amount and type of error and its consequences would appear to be characteristics of the disease, the physician, the patient, and the organizational setting in which diagnosis takes place. Thus for diseases such as pneumonia which produce almost certain impairment unless attended, and for which a quick and highly effective cure is available, the hypothesis is probably largely irrelevant. On the other hand, the hypothesis may be of considerable importance for diseases which have a less certain outcome, and for which existing treatments are protracted and of uncertain value. Mental disorders and some types of heart disease are cases in point.

The working philosophy of the physician is probably relevant to the predominant type of errors made. Physicians who generally favor active intervention probably make more Type 2 errors than physicians who view their treatments only as assistance for natural bodily reactions to disease. The physician's perception of the personality of the patient may also be relevant; Type 2 errors are less likely if the physician defines the patient as a "crock," a person overly sensitive to discomfort, rather than as a person who ignores or denies disease.

Finally, the organizational setting is relevant to the extent that it influences the relationship between the doctor and the patient. In some contexts, as in medical practice in organizations such as the military or industrial setting, the physician is not as likely to feel personal responsibility for the patient as he would in other contexts, such as private practice. This may be due in part to the conditions of financial remuneration, and perhaps equally important, the sheer volume of patients dependent on the doctor's time. Cultural or class differences may also affect the amount of social distance between doctor and patient, and therefore the amount of responsibility which the doctor feels for the patient. Whatever the sources, the more the physician feels personally responsible for the patient, the more likely he is to make a Type 2 error.

To the extent that future research can indicate the conditions which influence the amount, type, and consequences of error, such research can make direct contributions to medical practice. Three types of research seem necessary in order to establish the true risks of impairment associated with common disease signs. First, controlled field trials of treated and untreated outcomes in a normal population would be needed. Second, perhaps in conjunction with these field trials, experimental studies of the effect of suggestion of illness by physicians and others would be necessary to determine the risks of unnecessary entry into the sick role.

Finally, studies of a mathematical nature seem to be called for. Suppose that physicians were provided with the results of the studies suggested above. How could these findings be introduced into medical practice as a corrective to cultural and professional biases in decision-making procedures? One promising approach is the strategy of evaluating the relative utility of alternative courses of action, based upon decision theory or game theory.[24]

Ledley and Lusted reviewed a number of mathematical techniques which might be applicable to medical decision-making, one of these techniques being the use of the "expected value" equation, which is derived from game theory.[25] Although their discussion pertains to the relative value of two treatment procedures, it is also relevant, with only slight changes in wording, to determining the expected values of treatment relative to non-treatment. The expected values of two treatments, they say, may be calculated from a simple expression involving only two kinds of terms: the probability that the diagnosis is correct, and the absolute value of the treatment (at its simplest, the absolute value is the rate of cure for persons known to have the disease).

The "expected value" of a treatment is:

$$E_t = p_s v_s{}^s + (1 - p_s) v_h{}^s.$$

(The superscript refers to the way the patient is treated, the subscript refers to his actual conditions. s signifies sick, h, healthy.) That is, the expected value of a treatment is the probability p that the patient has the disease, multiplied by the value of the treatment for patients who actually have the disease, plus the probability that the patient does not have the disease $(1 - p)$, multiplied by the value (or "cost") of the treatment for patients who do not have the disease.

Similarly, the expected value of nontreatment is:

$$E_n = p_s v_s{}^h + (1 - p_s) v_h{}^h.$$

That is, the expected value of nontreatment is the prob-

24. H. Chernoff and L. E. Moses, *Elementary Decision Theory* (New York: Wiley, 1959).
25. R. S. Ledley and L. B. Lusted, "Reasoning Foundations of Medical Diagnosis," *Science*, 130 (1959), pp. 9-21.

ability that the patient has the disease multiplied by
the value (or "cost") of treating a person as healthy who
is actually sick, plus the probability that the patient does
not have the disease, multiplied by the value of not
treating a healthy person.

The best course of action is indicated by comparing
the magnitude of E_t and E_n. If E_t is larger, treatment
is indicated. If E_n is larger, nontreatment is indicated.
Evaluating these equations involves estimating the probability of correct diagnosis and constructing a payoff
matrix for the values of $v_s{}^s$ (proportion of patients who
actually had the disease who were cured by the treatment), $v_h{}^s$ (the cost of treating a healthy person as sick:
inconvenience, working days lost, surgical risks, unnecessary entry into sick role), $v_s{}^h$ (cost of treating a sick
person as well: a question involving the proportions of
persons who spontaneously recover, and the seriousness
of results when the disease goes unchecked), and finally,
$v_h{}^h$ (the value of not treating a healthy person: medical
expenses saved, working days, etc.).

To illustrate the use of the equation, Ledley and
Lusted assign *arbitrary* absolute values in a case, because,
as they say, "The decision of value problems frequently
involves intangibles such as moral and ethical standards
which must, in the last analysis, be left to the physician's
judgment."[26] One might argue, however, that it is better
to develop a technique for systematically determining
the absolute values of treatment and nontreatment, crude
though the technique might be, than to leave the problem to the perhaps refined, but nevertheless obscure,
judgment processes of the physician. Particularly in a
matter of comparing the value of treatment and non-
treatment, the problem is to avoid biases in the physi-

26. *Ibid.*, p. 16.

cian's judgment due to the kind of moral orientation discussed above.

It is possible, moreover, that the difficulty met by Ledley and Lusted is not that the factors to be evaluated are "intangibles," but that they are expressed in seemingly incommensurate units. How does one weigh the risk of death against the monetary cost of treatment? How does one weigh the risk of physical or social disability against the risk of death? Although these are difficult questions to answer, the idea of leaving them to the physician's judgment is probably not conducive to an understanding of the problem.

Following the lead of the economists in their studies of utility, it may be feasible to reduce the various factors to be weighed to a common unit. How could the benefits, costs, and risks of alternative acts in medical practice be expressed in monetary units? One solution might be to use payment rates in disability and life insurance, which offer a comparative evaluation of the "cost" of death, and permanent and temporary disability of various degrees. Although this approach does not include everything which physicians weigh in reaching decisions (pain and suffering cannot be weighed in this framework) it does include many of the major factors. It therefore would provide the opportunity of constructing a fairly realistic payoff matrix of absolute values, which would then allow for the determination of the relative value of treatment and nontreatment using the expected value equation.

Gathering data for the payoff matrix might make it possible to explore an otherwise almost inaccessible problem: the sometimes subtle conflicts of interest between the physician and the patient. Although it is fairly clear that medical intervention is unnecessary in particular cases, and that it is probably done for financial gain,[27] the evaluation of the influence of remuneration on diagnosis and treatment is probably in most cases a fairly intricate matter, requiring precise techniques of investigation. If the payoff were calculated in terms of values to the patient *and* values to the physician, such problems could be explored. Less tangible values such as convenience and work satisfactions could be introduced into the matrix. The following statements by psychiatrists were taken from Hollingshead and Redlich's study of social class and mental disorder:

"Seeing him every morning was a chore; I had to put him on my back and carry him for an hour." "He had to get attention in large doses, and this was hard to do." "The patient was not interesting or attractive; I had to repeat, repeat, repeat." "She was a poor unhappy, miserable woman—we were worlds apart."[28]

This study strongly suggests that psychiatric diagnosis and treatment are influenced by the payoff for the psychiatrist as well as for the patient. In any type of medical decision, the use of the expected value equation might show the extent of the conflict of interest between the physician and patient, and thereby shed light on the complex process of medical decision making.

27. R. E. Trussel, J. Ehrlich, and M. Morehead, *The Quantity, Quality and Costs of Medical and Hospital Care Secured by a Sample of Teamster Families in the New York Area* (New York: Columbia University School of Public Health and Administrative Medicine, 1962).

28. A. B. Hollingshead and F. C. Redlich, *Social Class and Mental Illness* (New York: Wiley, 1958), p. 344.

5

Two Studies

of the Societal Reaction

THE case for making the societal reaction to rule-breaking a major independent variable in studies of deviant behavior has been succinctly stated by Kitsuse:

A sociological theory of deviance must focus specifically upon the interactions which not only define behaviors as deviant but also organize and activate the application of sanctions by individuals, groups, or agencies. For in modern society, the socially significant differentiation of deviants from the nondeviant populations is increasingly contingent upon circumstances of situation, place, social and personal biography, and the bureaucratically organized activities of agencies of control.[1]

In the case of mental disorder, psychiatric diagnosis is one of the crucial steps which "organizes and activates" the societal reaction, since the state is legally empowered to segregate and isolate those persons whom psychiatrists find to be committable because of mental illness.

It has been argued here, however, that mental illness may be more usefully considered to be a social status than a disease, since the symptoms of mental illness are vaguely defined and widely distributed, and the definition of behavior as symptomatic of mental illness is

1. J. I. Kitsuse, "Societal Reaction to Deviant Behavior: Problems of Theory and Method," *Social Problems*, 9 (Winter, 1962), pp. 247-256.

usually dependent upon social rather than medical contingencies. Furthermore, the argument continues, the status of the mental patient is more often an ascribed status, with conditions for status entry and exit external to the patient, than an achieved status with conditions for status entry dependent upon the patient's own behavior.[2] According to this argument, the societal reaction is a fundamentally important variable in all stages of a deviant career.

The actual usefulness of a theory of mental disorder based on the societal reaction is largely an empirical question: to what extent is entry to and exit from the status of mental patient independent of the behavior or "condition" of the patient? This chapter will explore this question for two phases of the societal reaction: the legal and psychiatric screening of persons alleged to be mentally ill, and the decision to release patients resident in mental hospitals. These steps represent two of the official phases of the societal reaction, which occur after the alleged deviance has been called to the attention of the community. This chapter will make no reference to the initial rule-breaking or other situation which resulted in complaints, or to the behavior of patients after release, but will deal entirely with official decision procedures.

The purpose of the description that follows is to determine the extent of uncertainty that exists concerning patients' "qualifications" for involuntary confinement in a mental hospital and organizational reactions to this type of uncertainty. The data presented here indicate that, in the face of uncertainty, there is a strong pre-

2. The term status is used here in the sense of a socially acknowledged position in a group. For an introductory discussion of the concept of status, see L. Broom and P. Selznick, *Sociology* (New York: Harper and Row 1963), 3rd ed., p. 42.

sumption of illness by the court and the psychiatrists.[3] In the discussion that follows the presentation of findings, some of the causes, consequences and implications of the presumption of illness are suggested.

LEGAL AND PSYCHIATRIC SCREENING
OF INCOMING PATIENTS

The data upon which this phase of the study is based were drawn from psychiatrists' ratings of a sample of patients newly admitted to the public mental hospitals in a Midwestern state, official court records, interviews with court officials and psychiatrists, and our observations of psychiatric examinations in four courts.[4] The psychiatrists' ratings of new patients will be considered first.

In order to obtain a rough measure of the incoming patient's qualifications for involuntary confinement, a survey of newly admitted patients was conducted with the cooperation of the hospital psychiatrists. All psychiatrists who made admission examinations in the three large mental hospitals in the state filled out a questionnaire for the first ten consecutive patients they examined in the month of June 1962. A total of 223 questionnaires were returned by the 25 admission psychiatrists. Although these returns do not constitute a probability sample of all new patients admitted during the year, there were no obvious biases in the drawing of the sample. For this reason, this group of patients will be taken to be typical of the newly admitted patients in Midwestern State.

3. A general discussion of the presumption of illness is found in the first section of Chapter 4.
4. This phase of the study was completed with the assistance of Daniel M. Culver.

The two principal legal grounds for involuntary confinement in the United States are the police power of the state (the state's right to protect itself from dangerous persons) and *parens patriae* (the State's right to assist those persons who, because of their own incapacity, may not be able to assist themselves.)[5] As a measure of the first ground, the potential dangerousness of the patient, the questionnaire contained this item: "In your opinion, if this patient were released at the present time, is it likely he would harm himself or others?" The psychiatrists were given six options, ranging from Very Likely to Very Unlikely. Their responses were: Very Likely, 5 per cent; Likely, 4 per cent; Somewhat Likely, 14 per cent; Somewhat Unlikely, 20 per cent; Unlikely, 37 per cent; Very Unlikely, 18 per cent. (Three patients were not rated, 1 per cent).

As a measure of the second ground, *parens patriae*, the questionnaire contained the item: "Based on your observations of the patient's behavior, his present degree of mental impairment is:

None . . . Minimal . . . Mild . . . Moderate . . . Severe . . ."

The psychiatrists' responses were: None, 2 per cent; Minimal, 12 per cent; Mild, 25 per cent; Moderate, 42 per cent; Severe, 17 per cent. (Three patients were not rated, 1 per cent).

To be clearly qualified for involuntary confinement, a patient should be rated as likely to harm self or others (Very Likely, Likely, or Somewhat Likely), and/or as Severely Mentally Impaired. However, voluntary patients should be excluded from this analysis, since the court is not required to assess their qualifications for

---

5. H. A. Ross, "Commitment of the Mentally Ill: Problems of Law and Policy," *Michigan Law Review*, 57 (May, 1959), pp. 945-1018.

confinement. Excluding the 59 voluntary admissions (26 per cent of the sample) leaves a sample of 164 involuntarily confined patients. Of these patients, 10 were rated as meeting both qualifications for involuntary confinement, 21 were rated as being severely mentally impaired, but not dangerous, 28 were rated as dangerous but not severely mentally impaired, and 102 were rated as not dangerous nor as severely mentally impaired. (Three patients were not rated.)

According to these ratings, there is considerable uncertainty connected with the screening of newly admitted involuntary patients in the state, since a substantial majority (63 per cent) of the patients did not clearly meet the statutory requirements for involuntary confinement. How does the agency responsible for assessing the qualifications for confinement, the court, react in the large numbers of cases involving uncertainty?

On the one hand, the legal rulings on this point by higher courts are quite clear. They have repeatedly held that there should be a presumption of sanity. The burden of proof of insanity is to be on the petitioners, there must be a preponderance of evidence, and the evidence should be of a "clear and unexceptionable" nature.[6]

On the other hand, existing studies suggest that there is a presumption of illness by mental health officials. Mechanic describes admissions to two large mental hospitals located in an urban area in California in this way:

In the crowded state or county hospitals, which is the most typical situation, the psychiatrist does not have sufficient time to make a very complete psychiatric diagnosis, nor do his psychiatric tools provide him with the equipment for an expeditious screening of the patient. . . .

6. This is the typical phrasing in cases cited in *Decennial Legal Digest*, found under the heading "Mental Illness."

In the two mental hospitals studied over a period of three months, the investigator never observed a case where the psychiatrist advised the patient that he did not need treatment. Rather, all persons who appeared at the hospital were absorbed into the patient population regardless of their ability to function adequately outside the hospital.[7]

A comment by Brown suggests that it is a fairly general understanding among mental health workers that state mental hospitals in the United States accept all comers.[8] In a study of 58 commitment proceedings, Miller found that some of the proceedings were "routine rituals."[9]

Kutner, describing commitment procedures in Chicago in 1962, also reports a strong presumption of illness by the staff of the Cook County Mental Health Clinic:

Certificates are signed as a matter of course by staff physicians after little or no examination . . . The so-called examinations are made on an assembly-line basis, often being completed in two or three minutes, and never taking more than ten minutes. Although psychiatrists agree that it is practically impossible to determine a person's sanity on the basis of such a short and hurried interview, the doctors recommend confinement in 77 per cent of the cases. It appears in practice that the alleged-mentally-ill is presumed to be insane and bears the burden of proving his sanity in the few minutes allotted to him.[10]

These citations suggest that mental health officials handle uncertainty by presuming illness. Other investi-

7. D. Mechanic, "Some Factors in Identifying and Defining Mental Illness," *Mental Hygiene*, 46 (January, 1962), pp. 66-74.

8. E. L. Brown, *Newer Dimensions of Patient Care* (New York: Russell Sage Foundation, 1961), Part I, p. 60, footnote.

9. D. Miller, "County Lunacy Commission Hearings: Some Observations of Commitments to a State Mental Hospital," *Social Problems* (in press).

10. L. Kutner, "The Illusion of Due Process in Commitment Proceedings," *Northwestern University Law Review*, 57 (September, 1962), pp. 383-399.

gators, however, have reported conflicting findings.[11] To ascertain if the presumption of illness occurred in Midwestern State, intensive observations of screening procedures were conducted in the four courts with the largest volume of mental cases in the state. These courts were located in the two most populous cities in the state. Before giving the results of these observations, it is necessary to describe the steps in the legal procedures for hospitalization and commitment. The process of screening persons alleged to be mentally ill can be visualized as containing five steps in Midwestern State:

1. The application for judicial inquiry, made by three citizens. This application is heard by deputy clerks in two of the courts (C and D), by a court reporter in the third court, and by a court commissioner in the fourth court.
2. The intake examination, conducted by a hospital psychiatrist.
3. The psychiatric examination, conducted by two psychiatrists appointed by the court.
4. The interview of the patient by the guardian *ad litem*, a lawyer appointed in three of the courts to represent the patient. (Court A did not use guardians *ad litem*.)
5. The judicial hearing, conducted by a judge.

These five steps take place roughly in the order listed, although in many cases (those cases designated as

11. Lowenthal found in her study that the patient's condition was the most important determinant of hospitalization (M. F. Lowenthal, *Lives in Distress: Paths of the Elderly to the Psychiatric Ward* [New York: Basic Books, 1964]; Mishler and Waxler report that 39 per cent of applications to The Massachusetts Mental Health Center did not result in hospitalization, perhaps indicating that more rigorous screening was taking place (E. G. Mishler and N. E. Waxler, "Decision Processes in Psychiatric Hospitalization; Patients Referred, Accepted, and Admitted to a Psychiatric Hospital," *American Sociological Review*, 28 [August, 1963], pp. 576-587).

emergencies) step No. 2, the intake examination, may occur before step 1. Steps 1 and 2 usually take place on the same day or the day after hospitalization. Steps 3, 4, and 5 usually take place within a week of hospitalization. (In courts C and D, however, the judicial hearing is held only once a month.)

This series of steps would seem to provide ample opportunity for the presumption of health, and a thorough assessment, therefore, of the patient's qualifications for involuntary confinement, since there are five separate points at which discharge could occur. According to our findings, however, these procedures usually do not serve the function of screening out persons who do not meet statutory requirements. At most of these decision points, in most of the courts, retention of the patient in the hospital was virtually automatic. A notable exception to this pattern was found in one of the three state hospitals; this hospital attempted to use step No. 2, the intake examination, as a screening point to discharge patients that the superintendent described as "illegitimate," i.e., patients who do not qualify for involuntary confinement.[12] In the other two hospitals, however, this examination was perfunctory and virtually never resulted in a finding of health and a recommendation of discharge. In a similar manner, the other steps were largely ceremonial in character. For example, in court B, we observed twenty-two judicial hearings, all of which were conducted perfunctorily and with lightning rapidity. (The mean time of these hearings was 1.6 minutes.) The judge

12. Other exceptions occurred as follows: the deputy clerks in courts C and D appeared to exercise some discretion in turning away applications they considered improper or incomplete, at Step 1; the judge in Court D appeared also to perform some screening at Step 5. For further description of these exceptions, see the author's "Social Conditions for Rationality: How Urban and Rural Courts Deal with the Mentally Ill," *American Behavioral Scientist*, 7 (March, 1964), pp. 21-24.

asked each patient two or three routine questions: "How do you feel?" "How are you being treated?" "Would you cooperate with the doctors if they think you should stay awhile?" *Whatever* the patient's answer, however, the judge immediately ended the hearing, managing in this way to average less than two minutes per patient. Even if the patient was extremely outspoken, no attempt was made to accomodate him. The following excerpt from an official transcript provides an example of such a case:

J. "How are you, Miss ———?"

P. "Oh, pretty good."

J. "Are they treating you all right?"

P. "Yes."

J. "Any complaints?"

P. "No. The only complaint I have is that they won't let me out."

J. "Well, do you want to get out?"

P. "Sure."

J. "What if the doctors say you should stay for a while to get well?"

P. "Well, I don't see why I was sick, come in here in the first place."

J. "Well, let's see what the doctors say. Have they examined you yet—the doctors?"

P. "Well, examine me for what? For mental condition? I'm not mental as far as that is. The ones who brought me here—I think should be examined."

J. "Who brought you here?"

P. "The Police Department. Why, they come over to my house and they just grab people just like this. They try to make me say there is two tables when there is only one. What would you expect"

J. "All right, Miss ———."

P. "Where are your laws of today? I see that the laws are not very fair, not just either, or maybe your hospital needs money. We have to come here to help pay your bills . . ." (The patient had become quite angry.)

J. "Well, we are overcrowded now."

P. "Well, then where is your justice in this world today? You have none, the way it looks to me. I think better justice should be done with your Police Department and your authority . . ."

J. "All right, Miss ————, thank you."

P. "That's all I ask you to do. There are probably many like me today are facing the same problems that I do and they are not even guilty to be put up in a mental institution . . ."

J. "All right."

It should be noted that the judge made no attempt to inform this voluble patient of her right to counsel, which might have relieved her considerably. In this court, informing the patient of her rights was supposedly done through the guardian *ad litem*. The patient, however, had no way of knowing this at the time of the hearing.

Our observations of the guardian's interviews suggested, furthermore, that the guardians were not likely to take the patient's side, since, like the examining psychiatrists, they were paid a flat fee for each case. That is, their rate of pay depended on the rapidity with which they could finish. In recommending hospitalization, they were avoiding interruption of the already-occurring process of hospitalization and treatment; hence their interview could be quite short. If, on the other hand, they wished to recommend discharge, they would have to interrupt an on-going process, take the responsibility for such interruption, and build a case for discharge. Building such a case would have required considerably more time, thus severely reducing their rate of pay.

In the twelve interviews we observed by guardians, none of the guardians informed the patient of his rights. This omission was especially striking in the three interviews of one guardian, since he was quite vocal about the rights of the patients when interviewed beforehand:

Q: "What is the function of the guardian *ad litem*?"
A: "To protect the legal rights of the ward."
Q: "What are these rights?"
A: "*One*: trial by jury.
   Two: right to his own attorney.
   Three: right to a hearing.
   Four: right to petition for a re-examination.
   I think that the right to private counsel is very important."

Noticing that in none of the three cases did he inform the patient of any of the rights he quoted above, the interviewer asked him about the third case, in which this information might have been particularly useful to the patient.

Q: "I don't remember for sure, but did you tell John ———— (the last patient interviewed) about his right to a lawyer? Was this an oversight or did you skip it purposely?"
A: "I didn't purposely skip it so that he wouldn't know about it but I was conscious of not telling him. You know lawyers don't work for nothing and I had it in the back of my mind that Mr. ———— (the patient) was not able to pay for any lawyer because, as you remember, he said he had enough to get to Minneapolis. A guy hates to refer a client when he knows that client can't pay."

What appeared to be the key role in justifying these procedures was played in step No. 3, the examination by the court-appointed psychiatrists. In our informal discussions of screening with the judges, and other court officials, these officials made it clear that although the statutes give the court the responsibility for the decision to confine or release persons alleged to be mentally ill, they would rarely if ever take the responsibility for releasing a mental patient without a medical recommenda-

tion to that effect. The question which is crucial, therefore, for the entire screening process is whether or not the
court-appointed psychiatric examiners presume illness.
The remainder of the paper will consider this question.

Our observations of 116 judicial hearings raised the
question of the adequacy of the psychiatric examination.
Eighty-six of the hearings failed to establish that the
patients were "mentally ill" (according to the criteria
stated by the judges in interviews).[13] Indeed, the behavior and responses of 48 of the patients at the hearings
seemed completely unexceptionable. Yet the psychiatric
examiners had not recommended the release of a single
one of these patients. Examining the court records of 80
additional cases, we found still not a single recommendation for release.

Although the recommendation for treatment of 196
out of 196 consecutive cases strongly suggests that the
psychiatric examiners were presuming illness, particularly when we observed 48 of these patients to be responding appropriately, it is conceivable that this is not
the case. The observer for this study was not a psychiatrist (he was a first year graduate student in social work)
and it is possible that he could have missed evidence of
disorder which a psychiatrist might have seen. It was
therefore arranged for the observer to be present at a
series of psychiatric examinations, in order to determine
whether the examinations appeared to be merely formali-
ties or whether, on the other hand, through careful
examination and interrogation, the psychiatrists were able
to establish illness even in patients whose appearance
and responses were not obviously disordered. The ob-

13. In interviews with the judges, the following criteria were
named: appropriateness of behavior and speech, understanding of the
situation, and orientation.

server was instructed to note the examiner's procedures, the criteria they appeared to use in arriving at their decision, and their reaction to uncertainty.

Each of the courts discussed here employs the services of a panel of physicians as medical examiners. The physicians are paid a flat fee of ten dollars per examination, and are usually assigned from three to five patients for each trip to the hospital. In court A, most of the examinations are performed by two psychiatrists, who go to the hospital once a week, seeing from five to ten patients a trip. In court B, C, and D, a panel of local physicians is used. These courts seek to arrange the examinations so that one of the examiners is a psychiatrist, the other a general practitioner. Court B has a list of four such pairs, and appoints each pair for a month at a time. Courts C and D have a similar list, apparently with some of the same names as court B.

To obtain physicians who were representative of the panel used in these courts, we arranged to observe the examinations of the two psychiatrists employed by court A, and one of the four pairs of physicians used in court B, one a psychiatrist, the other a general practitioner. We observed 13 examinations in court A and 13 examinations in court B. The judges in courts C and D refused to give us the names of the physicians on their panels, and we were unable to observe examinations in these courts. (The judge in court D stated that he did not want these physicians harassed in their work, since it was difficult to obtain their services even under the best of circumstances.) In addition to observing the examinations by four psychiatrists, we interviewed three other psychiatrists used by these courts.

The medical examiners followed two lines of questioning. One line was to inquire about the circumstances which led to the patient's hospitalization, the other was to ask standard questions to test the patient's orientation and his capacity for abstract thinking by asking him the date, the President, Governor, proverbs, and problems requiring arithmetic calculation. These questions were often asked very rapidly, and the patient was usually allowed only a very brief time to answer.

It should be noted that the psychiatrists in these courts had access to the patient's record (which usually contained the Application for Judicial Inquiry and the hospital chart notes on the patient's behavior), and that several of the psychiatrists stated that they almost always familiarized themselves with this record before making the examination. To the extent that they were familiar with the patient's circumstances from such outside information, it is possible that the psychiatrists were basing their diagnosis of illness less on the rapid and peremptory examination than on this other information. Although this was true to some extent, the importance of the record can easily be exaggerated, both because of the deficiencies in the typical record, and because of the way it is usually utilized by the examiners.

The deficiencies of the typical record were easily discerned in the approximately one hundred applications and hospital charts which the author read. Both the applications and charts were extremely brief and sometimes garbled. Moreover, in some of the cases where the author and interviewer were familiar with the circumstances involved in the hospitalization, it was not clear that the complainant's testimony was any more accurate than the version presented by the patient. Often the original complaint was so paraphrased and condensed that the application seemed to have little meaning.

The attitude of the examiners toward the record was such that even in those cases where the record was ample, it often did not figure prominently in their decision. Disparaging remarks about the quality and usefulness of the record were made by several of the psychiatrists. One of the examiners was apologetic about his use of the record, giving us the impression that he thought that a good psychiatrist would not need to resort to any information outside his own personal examination of the patient. A casual attitude toward the record was openly displayed in 6 of the 26 examinations we observed. In these six examinations, the psychiatrist could not (or in three cases, did not bother to) locate the record and conducted the examination without it, with one psychiatrist making it a point of pride that he could easily diagnose most cases "blind."

In his observations of the examinations, the interviewer was instructed to rate how well the patient responded by noting his behavior during the interview, whether he answered the orientation and concept questions correctly, and whether he denied and explained the allegations which resulted in his hospitalization. If the patient's behavior during the interview obviously departed from conventional social standards (e.g., in one case the patient refused to speak), if he answered the orientation questions incorrectly, or if he did not deny and explain the petitioners' allegations, the case was rated as meeting the statutory requirements for hospitalization. Of the 26 examinations observed, eight were rated as "Criteria Met."

If, on the other hand, the patient's behavior was appropriate, his answers correct, and he denied and explained the petitioners' allegations, the interviewer rated the case as not meeting the statutory criteria. Of the 26 cases, seven were rated as "Criteria Not Met." Finally, if the examination was inconclusive, but the interviewer felt that more extensive investigation might have established that the criteria were met, he rated the cases as

"Criteria Possibly Met." Of the 26 examined, 11 were rated in this way. The interviewer was instructed that whenever he was in doubt to avoid using the rating "Criteria Not Met."

Even giving the examiners the benefit of the doubt, the interviewer's ratings were that a substantial majority of the examinations he observed failed to establish that the statutory criteria were met. The relationship between the examiners' recommendations and the interviewer's ratings are shown in Table 2.

TABLE 2
OBSERVER'S RATINGS AND EXAMINERS' RECOMMENDATIONS

Examiners' Recommendations	Observer's Ratings			
	Criteria Met	Criteria Possibly Met	Criteria Not Met	Total
Commitment	7	9	2	18
30-day Observation	1	2	3	6
Release	0	0	2	2
Total	8	11	7	26

The interviewer's ratings suggest that the examinations established that the statutory criteria were met in only 8 cases, but the examiners recommended that the patient be retained in the hospital in 24 cases, leaving 16 cases which the interviewer rated as uncertain, and in which retention was recommended by the examiners. The observed also rated the patient's expressed desires regarding staying in the hospital, and the time taken by the examination. The ratings of the patient's desire concerning staying or leaving the hospital were: Leave, 14 cases; Indifferent, 1 case; Stay, 9 cases; and Not Ascertained, 2 cases. In only one of the 14 cases in which the patient wished to leave was the interviewer's rating Criteria Met.

Interviews ranged in length from five minutes to 17 minutes, with the mean time being 10.2 minutes. Most of the interviews were hurried, with the questions of the examiners coming so rapidly that the examiner often interrupted the patient, or one examiner interrupted the other. All of the examiners seemed quite hurried. One psychiatrist, after stating in an interview (before we observed his examinations) that he usually took about thirty minutes, stated:

It's not remunerative. I'm taking a hell of a cut. I can't spend 45 minutes with a patient. I don't have the time, it doesn't pay.

In the eight examinations that we observed, this physician actually spent 8, 10, 5, 8, 8, 7, 17, and 11 minutes with the patients, or an average of 9.2 minutes.

In these short time periods, it is virtually impossible for the examiner to extend his investigation beyond the standard orientation questions and a short discussion of the circumstances which brought the patient to the hospital. In those cases where the patient answered the orientation questions correctly, behaved appropriately, and explained his presence at the hospital satisfactorily, the examiners did not attempt to assess the reliability of the petitioner's complaints, or to probe further into the patient's answers. Given the fact that in most of these instances the examiners were faced with borderline cases, that they took little time in the examinations, and that they usually recommended commitment, we can only conclude that their decisions were based largely on a presumption of illness. Supplementary observations reported by the interviewer support this conclusion.

After each examination, the observer asked the examiner to explain the criteria he used in arriving at his decision. The observer also had access to the examiner's official report, so that he could compare what the examiner said about the case with the record of what actually occurred during the interview. This supplementary information supports the conclusion that the examiner's decisions are based on the presumption of illness, and sheds light on the manner in which these decisions are reached:

1. The "evidence" upon which the examiners based their decision to retain often seemed arbitrary.
2. In some cases, the decision to retain was made even when no evidence could be found.
3. Some of the psychiatrists' remarks suggest prejudgment of the cases.
4. Many of the examinations were characterized by carelessness and haste.

The first question, concerning the arbitrariness of the psychiatric evidence, will now be considered. In the weighing of the patient's responses during the interview, the physician appeared not to give the patient credit for the large number of correct answers he gave. In the typical interview, the examiner might ask the patient fifteen or twenty questions: the date, time, place, who is President, Governor, etc., what is 11×10, 11×11, etc., explain "Don't put all your eggs in one basket," "A rolling stone gathers no moss," etc. The examiners appeared to feel that a wrong answer established lack of orientation, even when it was preceded by a series of correct answers. In other words, the examiners do not establish any standard score on the orientation questions, which would give an objective picture of the degree to which the patient answered the questions correctly, but seem at times to search until they find an incorrect answer.

For those questions which were answered incorrectly, it was not always clear whether the incorrect answers were due to the patient's "mental illness," or to the time pressure in the interview, the patient's lack of education, or other causes. Some of the questions used to establish orientation were sufficiently difficult that persons not mentally ill might have dificulty with them. Thus one of the examiners always asked, in a rapid-fire manner: "What year is it?" What year was it seven years ago? Seventeen years before that?" etc. Only two of the five patients who were asked this series of questions were able to answer it correctly. However, it is a moot question whether a higher percentage of persons in a household survey would be able to do any better. To my knowledge, none of the orientation questions that are used have been checked in a normal population.

Finally, the interpretations of some of the evidence as showing mental illness seemed capricious. Thus one of the patients, when asked, "In what ways are a banana, an orange, and an apple alike?" answered, "They are all something to eat." This answer was used by the examiner in explaining his recommendation to commit. The observer had noted that the patient's behavior and responses seemed appropriate and asked why the recommendation to commit had been made. The doctor stated that her behavior had been bizarre (possibly referring to her alleged promiscuity), her affect inappropriate ("When she talked about being pregnant, it was without feeling,") and with regard to the question above: "She wasn't able to say a banana and an orange were fruit. She couldn't take it one step further, she had to say it was something to eat." In other words, this psychiatrist was suggesting that in her thinking the patient manifested concreteness, which is held to be a symptom of mental illness. Yet in her other answers to classification questions, and to proverb interpretations, concreteness was not apparent, suggesting that the examiner's application of this test was arbitrary. In another case, the physician stated that he thought the patient was suspicious and distrustful, because he had asked about the possibility of being represented by counsel at the judicial hearing. The observer felt that these and other similar interpretations might possibly be correct, but that further investigation of the supposedly incorrect responses would be needed to establish that they were manifestations of disorientation.

In several cases where even this type of evidence was not available, the examiners still recommended retention in the hospital. Thus, one examiner employed by court A stated that he had recommended 30-day observation for a patient whom he had thought *not* to be mentally ill, on the grounds that the patient, a young man, could not get along with his parents, and "might get into trouble." This examiner went on to say:

We always take the conservative side (commitment or observation). Suppose a patient should commit suicide. We always make the conservative decision. I had rather play it safe. There's no harm in doing it that way.

It appeared to the observer that "playing safe" meant that even in those cases where the examination established nothing, the psychiatrists did not consider recommending release. Thus in one case the examination had established that the patient had a very good memory, was oriented, and spoke quietly and seriously. The observer recorded his discussion with the physician after the examination as follows:

When the doctor told me he was recommending commitment for

this patient too (he had also recommended commitment in the two examinations held earlier that day) he laughed because he could see what my next question was going to be. He said, "I already recommended the release of two patients this month." This sounded like it was the maximum amount the way he said it.

Apparently this examiner felt that he had a very limited quota on the number of patients he could recommend for release (less than 2 per cent of those examined).

The language used by these physicians tends to intimate that mental illness was found, even when reporting the opposite. Thus in one case the recommendation stated: "No gross evidence of delusions or hallucinations." This statement is misleading, since not only was there no gross evidence, there was not any evidence, not even the slightest suggestion of delusions or hallucinations, brought out by the interview.

These remarks suggest that the examiners prejudge the cases they examine. Several further comments indicate prejudgment. One physician stated that he thought that most crimes of violence were committed by patients released too early from mental hospitals. (This is an erroneous belief.[14]) He went on to say that he thought that all mental patients should be kept in the hospital at least three months, indicating prejudgment concerning his examinations. Another physician, after a very short interview (8 minutes), told the observer:

On the schizophrenics, I don't bother asking them more questions when I can see they're schizophrenic because *I know what they are going to say.* You could talk to them another half hour and not learn any more.

Another physician, finally, contrasted cases in which the patient's family or others initiated hospitalization ("pe-

14. See footnote 16, Chapter 3.

tition cases," the great majority of cases) with those cases initiated by the court:

The petition cases are pretty *automatic*. If the patient's own family wants to get rid of him you know there is something wrong.

The lack of care which characterized the examinations is evident in the forms on which the examiners make their recommendations. On most of these forms, whole sections have been left unanswered. Others are answered in a peremptory and uninformative way. For example, in the section entitled "Physical Examination," the question is asked: "Have you made a physical examination of the patient? State fully what is the present physical condition." A typical answer is "Yes. Fair.," or "Is apparently in good health." Since in none of the examinations we observed was the patient actually physically examined, these answer appear to be mere guesses. One of the examiners used regularly in court B, to the question "On what subject or in what way is derangement now manifested?" always wrote in "Is mentally ill." The omissions, and the almost flippant brevity of these forms, together with the arbitrariness, lack of evidence, and prejudicial character of the examinations, discussed above, all support the observer's conclusion that, except in very unusual cases, the psychiatric examiner's recommendation to retain the patient is virtually automatic.

Lest it be thought that these results are unique to a particularly backward Midwestern State, it should be pointed out that this state is noted for its progressive psychiatric practices. It will be recalled that a number of the psychiatrists employed by the court as examiners had finished their psychiatric residencies, which is not always the case in many other states. A still common practice in other states is to employ, as members of the

"Lunacy Panel," partially retired physicians with no psychiatric training whatever. This was the case, in 1959, in Stockton, California, where I observed hundreds of hearings at which these physicians were present. It may be indicative of some of the larger issues underlying the question of civil commitment that, in these hearings, the physicians played very little part; the judge controlled the questioning of the relatives and patients, and the hearings were often a model of impartial and thorough investigation.

Ratings of the qualifications for involuntary confinement of patients newly admitted to the public mental hospitals in a Midwestern state, together with observations of judicial hearings and psychiatric examinations by the observer connected with the present study, suggest that the decision as to the mental condition of a majority of the patients is an uncertain one. The fact that the courts seldom release patients, and the perfunctory manner in which the legal and medical procedures are carried out, suggest that the judicial decision to retain patients in the hospital for treatment is routine and largely based on the presumption of illness. Three reasons for this presumption will be discussed: financial, ideological, and political.

Our discussions with the examiners indicated that one reason that they perform biased "examinations" is that their rate of pay is determined by the length of time spent with the patient. In recommending retention, the examiners are refraining from interrupting the hospitalization and commitment procedures already in progress, and thereby allowing someone else, usually the hospital, to make the effective decision to release or commit. In order to recommend release, however, they would have to build a case showing why these procedures should be interrupted. Building such a case would take much more time than is presently expended by the examiners, thereby reducing their rate of pay.

A more fundamental reason for the presumption of illness by the examiners, and perhaps the reason why this practice is allowed by the courts, is the interpretation of current psychiatric doctrine by the examiners and court officials. These officials make a number of assumptions, which are now thought to be of doubtful validity:

1. The condition of mentally ill persons deteriorates rapidly without psychiatric assistance.

2. Effective psychiatric treatments exist for most mental illnesses.

3. Unlike surgery, there are no risks involved in involuntary psychiatric treatment: it either helps or is neutral, it can't hurt.

4. Exposing a prospective mental patient to questioning, cross-examination, and other screening procedures exposes him to the unnecessary stigma of trial-like procedures, and may do further damage to his mental condition.

5. There is an element of danger to self or others in most mental illness. It is better to risk unnecessary hospitalization than the harm the patient might do himself or others.

Many psychiatrists and others now argue that none of these assumptions are necessarily correct.

1. The assumption that psychiatric disorders usually get worse without treatment rests on very little other than evidence of an anecdotal character. There is just as much evidence that most acute psychological and emotional upsets are self-terminating.[15]

15. For a review of epidemiological studies of mental disorder, see R. J. Plunkett and J. E. Gordon, *Epidemiology and Mental Illness* (New York: Basic Books, 1960). Most of these studies suggest that at

2. It is still not clear, according to systematic studies evaluating psychotherapy, drugs, etc., that most psychiatric interventions are any more effective, on the average, than no treatment at all.[16]

3. There is very good evidence that involuntary hospitalization and social isolation may affect the patient's life: his job, his family affairs, etc. There is some evidence that too hasty exposure to psychiatric treatment may convince the patient that he is "sick," prolonging what might have been an otherwise transitory episode.[17]

4. This assumption is correct, as far as it goes. But it is misleading because it fails to consider what occurs when the patient who does not wish to be hospitalized is forcibly treated. Such patients often become extremely indignant and angry, particularly in the case, as often happens, when they are deceived into coming to the hospital on some pretext.

5. The element of danger is usually exaggerated both in amount and degree. In the psychiatric survey of new patients in state mental hospitals, danger to self or others was mentioned in about a fourth of the cases. Furthermore, in those cases where danger is mentioned, it is not

---

any given point in time, psychiatrists find a substantial proportion of persons in normal populations to be "mentally ill." One interpretation of this finding is that much of the deviance in these studies is self-limiting.

16. For an assessment of the evidence regarding the effectiveness of electroshock, drugs, psychotherapy and other psychiatric treatments, see H. J. Eysenck, *Handbook of Abnormal Psychology* (New York: Basic Books, 1961), Part III.

17. For examples from military psychiatry, see A. J. Glass, "Psychotherapy in the Combat Zone," in *Symposium on Stress* (Washington, D.C., Army Medical Service, Graduate School, 1953), and B. L. Bushard, "The U.S. Army's Mental Hygiene Consultation Service," in *Symposium on Preventive and Social Psychiatry* (Washington, D.C.: Walter Reed Army Institute of Research, 1957), pp. 431-443. For a discussion of essentially the same problem in the context of a civilian mental hospital, *cf.* Kai T. Erikson, "Patient Role and Social Uncertainty—A Dilemma of the Mentally Ill," *Psychiatry*, 20 (August, 1957), pp. 263-274.

always clear that the risks involved are greater than those encountered in ordinary social life. This issue has been discussed by Ross, an attorney:

A truck driver with a mild neurosis who is "accident prone" is probably a greater danger to society than most psychotics; yet, he will not be committed for treatment, even if he would be benefited. The community expects a certain amount of dangerous activity. I suspect that as a class, drinking drivers are a greater danger than the mentally ill, and yet the drivers are tolerated or punished with small fines rather than indeterminate imprisonment.[18]

From our observations of the medical examinations and other commitment procedures, we formed a very strong impression that the doctrines of danger to self or others, early treatment, and the avoidance of stigma were invoked partly because the officials believed them to be true, and partly because they provided convenient justification for a preexisting policy of summary action, minimal investigation, avoidance of responsibility and, after the patient is in the hospital, indecisiveness and delay.

The policy of presuming illness is probably both cause and effect of political pressure on the court from the community. The judge, an elected official, runs the risk of being more heavily penalized for erroneously releasing than for erroneously retaining patients. Since the judge personally appoints the panel of psychiatrists to serve as examiners, he can easily transmit the community pressure to them, by failing to reappoint a psychiatrist whose examinations were inconveniently thorough.

Some of the implications of these findings for the sociology of deviant behavior will be briefly summarized. The foregoing discussion of the reasons that the psychiatrists tend to presume illness suggests that the motivations of the key decision-makers in the screening process

18. Ross, *op. cit.*, p. 962.

may be significant in determining the extent and direction of the societal reaction. In the case of psychiatric screening of persons alleged to be mentally ill, the social differentiation of the deviant from the nondeviant population appears to be materially affected by the financial, ideological, and political position of the psychiatrists, who are in this instance the key agents of social control.

Under these circumstances, the character of the societal reaction appears to undergo a marked change from the pattern of denial which occurs in the community. The official societal reaction appears to reverse the presumption of normality reported by the Cummings as a characteristic of informal societal reaction, and instead exaggerates both the amount and degree of deviance.[19] Thus, one extremely important contingency influencing the severity of the societal reaction may be whether or not the original rule-breaking comes to official notice. This paper suggests that in the area of mental disorder, perhaps in contrast to other areas of deviant behavior, if the official societal reaction is invoked, for whatever reason, social differentiation of the deviant from the nondeviant population will usually occur.

This section has sought to demonstrate that the behavior or "condition" of the person alleged to be mentally ill is not usually an important factor in the decision of officials to retain or release new patients from the mental hospital. The marginal nature of the majority of the cases, the peremptoriness and inadequacy of most of the examinations, when considered in light of the fact that virtually every patient is recommended for commitment, would appear to demonstrate this proposition. Additional illustrative material was discussed which also supported

19. E. and J. Cumming, *Closed Ranks* (Cambridge, Mass: Harvard University Press, 1957), p. 102.

this conclusion. The next section is a discussion of a study of the release of patients after they have been treated.

RELEASE OF PATIENTS:
PSYCHIATRIC AND SOCIAL CONTINGENCIES

In this discussion we have sought to formulate questions concerning mental disorder in such a way that research and discussion in this area could be integrated into the general body of sociological theory. That is, we have considered the mental patient to be a person occupying a special status in the social structure. Viewed in this way, questions concerning the course of treated "mental illness" become problems of status mobility: diagnosis and cure become, sociologically, entry and exit to and from the status of a mental patient. Since a career may be viewed as the occupancy of a status over a period of time, questions concerning the conditions under which confinement in a mental hospital is initiated and terminated become questions of "career contingencies."

The contingency which is usually considered to be determinate in the mobility of mental patients is the psychiatric condition of the patient himself. The status of the mental patient, that is, is considered to be an achieved status, dependent only on the patient's behavior. We have argued, however, that the mental patient's status is partly ascribed. Lemert points to the putative character of the societal reaction, and Goffman states:[20]

The society's official view is that inmates of mental hospitals are there primarily because they are suffering from mental illness. However, in the degree that the "mentally ill" outside hospitals

20. Lemert, *op. cit.*, pp. 55-56; Goffman, *op. cit.*, p. 135.

numerically approach or surpass those inside hospitals, one could say that mental patients distinctively suffer not from mental illness, but from contingencies.

This passage suggests the hypothesis that contingencies external to the patient (such as the number of hospital beds available, the willingness of the community to accept a patient that the hospital wishes to discharge, etc.) may be as fateful for a patient's career as the hospital's evaluation of his medical and legal qualification for confinement.

The results of the numerous prior studies of the relationship between the social and psychiatric characteristics of patients, and release, do not appear to be useful in evaluating the hypothesis that social and situational characteristics may be crucial in release. These studies consistently show a relationship between social variables and release rates, without, however, controlling for the patients' qualifications for release.[21] It is thus not clear, (using class as an example) whether lower class patients have poorer chances for release because they are less qualified, or because class, independently of qualifications, somehow determines release chances. This ambiguity, which runs like a thread through most of the literature on social medicine, is also characteristic of studies of the release of mental patients.

21. One such study (E. L. Linn, "Patients' Socioeconomic Characteristics and Release from a Mental Hospital," *American Journal of Sociology*, 65 [November, 1959], pp. 280-286) cites other representative studies (see footnote 4, p. 281). Two studies with a different approach but the same limitations are O. G. Simmons, J. A. Davis, and K. Spencer, "Interpersonal Strains in Release from a Mental Hospital," *Social Problems*, 4 (July, 1956), pp. 21-28, and J. E. Freeman and O. G. Simmons, "Consensus and Coalition in the Release of Mental Patients: A Research Note," *Human Organization*, 20 (Summer, 1961), pp. 89-91. The study by Dinitz *et al.* is an exception to this statement; their results support the theory discussed here (see Dinitz *et al.*, footnote 41, Chapter 3).

This section seeks to test the hypothesis that social contingencies may be crucial, by examining the joint effect of social and psychiatric contingencies on release plans for mental patients in a Midwestern state. If mental patients "distinctively suffer not from mental illness, but from contingencies," we would expect to find that the decision to release or retain can be explained in terms of the patient's condition for only some of the patients, and that for the remainder, contingencies such as type of hospital, the patient's age, and his length of confinement must be introduced.[22]

The data used in this study were obtained through standard questionnaires distributed to the staff of all public mental hospitals in a Midwestern state. On June 1, 1962, a 4 per cent systematic sample ($N=555$) of patients was drawn from lists which comprised the entire patient population in the state, 13,684 persons at the time the sample was drawn. (Hospitals for the criminally insane and mentally retarded were not included.) Of the 555 questionnaires distributed, 4 were not returned, and 21 patients were checked as released (10), transferred (3), or died (8) during the period (about two weeks) between the drawings of the sample and the interviewing of the patients, leaving a total sample of 530 cases.

The hospital official legally responsible for the patient (a psychiatrist, social worker, or hospital superintendent) interviewed each patient whose name fell into the sample, and filled out the questionnaire on the basis of the interview and other knowledge he had of the patient. A total of 63 officials participated in the study by returning these questionnaires. The questionnaire contained 24 questions about the patient's history and

22. Of the social characteristics included in the questionnaire, these three were most strongly associated with release plans.

his present condition, and included questions about the examiner's rating of the patient's degree of mental impairment, the likelihood the patient would harm himself or others if released, personal characteristics such as the patient's age, sex, education, usual occupation, etc. and whether or not the hospital was making plans for releasing the patient. Before discussing the relationship between release plans and contingencies, I will give a brief description of the characteristics of the patients in the sample.

The ratings of the patient's education and usual occupation suggest that the hospital population is comprised mostly of persons of low social class: only 15 per cent of the patients in the sample had completed high school, and only a third of these had one or more years of college. Four per cent of the patients had professional, managerial, or technical, usual occupations, and 5 per cent clerical and sales, the rest of the sample falling into manual and farm labor classification, and non-labor-force. Twenty-eight per cent of the patients were rated as being first admissions. A simple check of the proportion male in the sample against the proportion male in the total hospital population fails to show bias in the sampling and questionnaire collection: 50 per cent of the patients in the sample were male, which is the same proportion reported in the total census by the Midwest State division of mental hospitals for the month in which the survey was conducted.

Release plans were reported for 43 of the patients (8 per cent of the total sample). One important contingency which would be expected to influence the number of release plans is type of hospital. In Midwestern State, public mental hospitals may be classified into two categories: receiving hospitals, where most first admissions are brought, and transfer hospitals, whose patient populations are largely made up of persons transferred from the receiving hospitals. The receiving hospitals appear to be, on the whole, more treatment and release-oriented than the transfer hospitals. All three of the receiving hospitals maintained staffs of full-time psychiatrists, psychologists, and social workers. Most of the transfer hospitals, however, maintained only a single social worker or a part-time or consulting psychiatrist. The responses to one item on the questionnaire concerning treatment show, for example, that 27 per cent of the patients in the transfer hospitals received no form of treatment whatever, except "custodial care." In the receiving hospitals, only 15 per cent of the patients were rated as receiving no treatment.

The amount of release planning in the receiving hospitals also exceeds that in the transfer hospitals, as shown in Table 3.

TABLE 3

RELEASE PLANS IN RECEIVING AND TRANSFER HOSPITALS

	Receiving	Transfer	Total
	(28%)	(3%)	
Release Plans	31	12	43
No Release Plans	76	403	479
Not Ascertained	2	6	8
Total	109	421	530

This table indicates a substantial difference in the proportion of release plans between the two types of hospitals: 28 per cent for the receiving hospitals, but only 3 per cent for the transfer hospitals. This difference could be interpreted to mean that patients in the transfer hospitals have considerably less chance for release than those in receiving hospitals, simply because they happen to be in transfer hospitals. An alternative interpretation, however, is that the patients in the transfer hospitals are less qualified for release. Before making any interpretation, knowledge of the qualifications of each group of patients for release is necessary.

Two items on the questionnaire are relevant to the patients' qualifications for release. (The same items were used in the first study in this chapter, cf. p. 130.) The first item concerns the potential harm the patient might commit if released: "In your opinion, if this patient were released at the present time, is it likely that he would harm himself or others?" The examiner was allowed six options in answering, ranging from Very Likely to Very Unlikely. The responses to this question were as follows: Very Likely, 6 per cent; Likely, 9.2 per cent; Somewhat Likely, 12.2 per cent; Somewhat Unlikely, 17.9 per cent; Unlikely, 32.8 per cent; Very Unlikely, 20.8 per cent (No rating, 0.6 per cent).

The second item relevant to patients' qualifications for release concerned the degree of mental impairment: "Based on your observations of the patient's behavior, his present degree of mental impairment is: None, Minimal, Mild, Moderate, or Severe." The responses were 0.6 per cent, 4.5 per cent, 18.7 per cent, 45.0 per cent, and 30.8 per cent, respectively, and .6 per cent not rated.

These two ratings, taken together, may be used as a measure of the patient's qualification for release, since likelihood of harm and degree of mental impairment correspond roughly to the two principle legal justifications for involuntary confinement: the police power of the state to protect itself against harm, and *parens patriae*, the right of the state to assist those, who because of incapacity, may be unable to assist themselves. (A fuller discussion of this point is found on page 130.[23]) Those patients rated as likely to harm themselves or

23. Ross, *op. cit.*

others if released will be considered as not qualified for release, by reason of the police power. Those patients rated as severely mentally impaired will be considered to be not qualified for release by reason of *parens patriae*.

It may be objected that survey questions concerning degree of danger and mental impairment are overly simple and perhaps unreliable instruments for assessing the complex issues involved in estimating the patient's condition. It should be noted, however, that the psychiatrist or other official who answered the questions about the patient is the person *legally responsible* for the patient's welfare, and is therefore in a position to give more than a casual evaluation. Although likelihood of danger and degree of mental impairment are admittedly only crude indices, these indices were administered in a uniform way (i.e., as questions on a standard questionnaire), they have face validity, and have never been demonstrated to be unreliable. In these respects, the indices compare favorably with the more traditional measure of the patient's condition, his psychiatric diagnosis. Psychiatric diagnoses are not made in a rigidly uniform manner, they do not have face validity, and they have been repeatedly demonstrated to be unreliable.[24] Under these conditions, the indices of danger and degree of mental impairment yield the best available estimate of the patient's qualifications for release.

The relationship between release plans and qualifications for release can be determined by noting the proportion of release plans within each impairment category, after excluding those cases which were rated as likely to harm themselves or others. Twenty cases from the receiving hospital sample and 129 cases from the transfer

24. For a recent review, see A. T. Beck, "Reliability of Psychiatric Diagnoses: 1. A Critique of Systematic Studies," *American Journal of Psychiatry*, 119 (September, 1962), pp. 210-216.

hospital sample were rated as likely to harm themselves
or others if released, or not rated. (There were release
plans for one patient in each of these two groups.) Table 4 shows the relationship between degree of mental
impairment and release plans for the remainder of the
sample, those patients rated as not likely to harm themselves or others.

TABLE 4

RELEASE PLANS AND MENTAL IMPAIRMENT OF PATIENTS
RATED NOT LIKELY TO HARM THEMSELVES OR OTHERS*

Receiving Hospitals
Degree of Impairment

	None or Min.	Mild	Mod.	Severe	T
Release Plans	(100%) 5	(55%) 16	(21%) 8	(07%) 1	30
No Release Plans	0	13	30	14	57
Total	5	29	38	15	87

Transfer Hospitals
Degree of Impairment

	None or Min.	Mild	Mod.	Severe	NA	T
Release Plans	(29%) 5	(7%) 4	(2%) 2	(0%) 0	0	11
No Release Plans	12	52	122	86	3	275
Total	17	56	124	86	3	286

* Omitted from this table are 148 patients rated as likely to harm
self or others, and 9 patients who were not rated as to release plans or
likelihood of harm.

This table shows that there is a very strong association between release plans and impairment in the receiving hospitals; the proportion of patients for whom there are release plans drops from 100 per cent in the category "None or Minimal Impairment" to 7 per cent in the category "Severe Impairment." In the transfer hospitals, the association is much weaker: of those patients rated in the categories "None or Minimal Impairment," only 29 per cent were reported with release plans. The proportion drops to 0 per cent for those patients rated as severely impaired. The fact that the differences between release plans in the receiving and transfer hospitals does not disappear when patient qualifications for release are introduced suggests that social contingencies (such as the patient's financial status, the availability of nursing homes, etc.) may be important in release.

Two contingencies which may be related to the differing rates of release plans are the age and length of confinement of the patients in each type of hospital, as shown in Table 5. Fifty-five per cent of the patients in the transfer hospital sample were over 60 years of age, and only 10 per cent of the patients in the receiving hospital were older than 60. Fifty-three per cent of the patients in the transfer hospitals have been confined for ten years or longer, and only 18 per cent of the patients in the receiving hospital have been confined for this long. It is conceivable that the ages and lengths of confinement of the patients, rather than differences in release policies, may account for the difference in the release plans rates.

One way of determining the effect of age and length of confinement on release is to determine if patients over 60 or those who have been confined for longer than ten years are over-represented in the group of "qualified" patients for whom there are no release plans. In the receiving hospital sample this is not the case: patients over

TABLE 5

AGE AND LENGTH OF CONFINEMENT OF PATIENTS IN
RECEIVING AND TRANSFER HOSPITALS

Receiving Hospitals
Length of Confinement

Age	Less than 10 Years	10 Years or More	T
Under 60	(78%) 85	(12%) 13	98
60 or more	(4%) 4	(6%) 7	11
Totals			109 (100%)

Transfer Hospitals
Length of Confinement

Age	Less than 10 Years	10 Years or More	T
Under 60	(21%) 87	(25%) 104	191
60 or more	(26%) 111	(28%) 119	230
Totals			421 (100%)

TABLE 6

AGE AND LENGTH OF CONFINEMENT OF QUALIFIED PATIENTS
FOR WHOM THERE ARE NO RELEASE PLANS

Age	Length of Confinement			
	Receiving Hospitals		Transfer Hospitals	
	Less than 10 Years	10 Years or More	Less than 10 Years	10 Years or More
Under 60	(76%) 32	(10%) 4	(23%) 43	(46%) 85
60 or more	(5%) 2	(10%) 4	(17%) 31	(15%) 27
Totals	42 (100%)		186 (100%)	

60, or confined longer than 10 years, or both, represent only 5 per cent, 9.5 per cent and 9.5 per cent respectively, of the group of qualified patients for whom there are no release plans ($N=42$). These are roughly the same proportions as these age and confinement groups in the total receiving hospital sample.

In the transfer hospital sample, however, patients confined more than 10 years are overrepresented in the group of qualified patients for whom there are no release plans. Patients over 60, or confined longer than 10 years, or both, constitute 17 per cent, 46 per cent and 15 per cent respectively, of the qualified patients for whom there are no release plans but 25 per cent, 26 per cent, and 28 per cent of the total transfer hospitals sample. Since the proportion of patients under 60 years of age, but confined longer than 10 years is almost twice as great among the qualified patients for whom there are no release plans, than it is in the sample as a whole, length of confinement is suggested as an important contingency for release in the transfer hospitals.

If a shorter length of confinement (2 years) is taken as a cutting point, the effect of length of confinement on release plans can be seen even in the treatment and release-oriented receiving hospitals. In Table 7, the relationship between release plans and impairment for short and long-term patients in the receiving hospitals is shown. (As in the prior table, the 20 patients rated as likely to harm themselves or others are excluded, as are two patients for whom length of confinement was not ascertained.) According to Table 7, for those patients (rated as unlikely to harm themselves or others) who have been in the receiving hospitals for less than two years, there are release plans for 72 per cent of the slightly impaired, and 16 per cent of the moderately and severely impaired. For those patients who had been in the receiving hos-

TABLE 7

RELEASE PLANS, DEGREE OF MENTAL IMPAIRMENT AND LENGTH OF
HOSPITALIZATION FOR PATIENTS IN RECEIVING HOSPITALS SAMPLE
WHO WERE RATED AS UNLIKELY TO HARM THEMSELVES
OR OTHERS

Length of Hospitalization 0-2 years

| | Degree of Mental Impairment | | |
	None Min. Mild	*Moderate or Severe*	*T*
Release Plans	(72%) 15	(16%) 6	21
No Release Plans	6	32	38
Totals	21	38	59

Length of Hospitalization 2 or more years

| | Degree of Mental Impairment | | |
	None Min. Mild	*Moderate or Severe*	*T*
Release Plans	(46%) 6	(20%) 3	9
No Release Plans	7	12	19
Totals	13	15	28

pitals for more than two years, there are release plans
for only 46 per cent of the slightly impaired and for 20
per cent of the moderately and severely impaired. The
proportion of patients for whom there were release plans
is very low for patients rated as moderately or severely
impaired, in both the short and long-term groups. For
the slightly impaired, however, the proportion of patients
for whom there were release plans drops from 72 per
cent of the short term patients to 46 per cent of the long-
term patients, suggesting that release chances decrease
for long-term patients, whatever their qualifications for

release. This finding provides support for the idea current among mental health workers that long confinement can, in itself, reduce patients' chances for discharge.

This section has presented data to test the hypothesis that social, rather than psychiatric contingencies may be crucial in release plans for mental patients. Ratings of the likelihood that patients would harm themselves or others if released, and ratings of the degree of mental impairment were employed as indices of psychiatric contingencies. The social contingencies were type of hospital, age, and length of continuous confinement.

The findings strongly support the initial hypothesis. The treatment and release-oriented receiving hospital were found to have a much greater proportion of release plans than the custody-oriented transfer hospitals. This difference does not disappear when differences in the qualifications of the patients are introduced. The majority of patients who appear qualified for release from a medical and legal point of view, but for whom there are no release plans, are patients whose age or length of confinement appear to be significant contingencies. Since age and long confinement would tend to make patients dependent on their families and community, the importance of these variables suggest that the community's acceptance of its former members may be a crucial contingency in release.[25]

The data presented here indicate that there is a large

25. The effect of the community's attitude is increased in those hospitals that maintain an informal policy of retaining marginal patients unless someone in the community is willing to take the responsibility for them. The existence of such policies was noted in Gainford's comments on *Report on Texas Hospitals and Institutions* (Austin, Texas: Texas Research League, 1956): "In Texas, as in other states, it was a rule in state hospitals that no patient could be released unless he had a place to go to.'" (John Gainford, "How Texas is Reforming its Mental Hospitals," *The Reporter*, 15 (November 20, 1956), pp. 18-22).

proportion of the patient population, 43 per cent, whose presence in the hospital cannot readily be explained in terms of their psychiatric condition. Their presence suggests the putative character of the societal reaction to deviance, and that for at least a near-majority of the patients, their status is largely ascribed rather than achieved. All of the findings taken together point to the usefulness of an analysis of career contingencies in the social mobility of mental patients, quite distinct from considerations of the dynamics of "mental illness."

6

THIS final chapter will recapitulate the theory and research that has been discussed, and add two final suggestions: a recommendation concerning interpretation of psychiatric symptoms, which has implications for research on mental illness, and a theoretical formulation in which the investigation of the causes of mental illness is translated into a study of the dynamics of status systems.

The theory of mental illness outlined in the earlier chapters is that the symptoms of mental illness can be considered to be violations of residual social norms, and that the careers of residual deviants can most effectively be considered as dependent on the societal reaction and the processes of role-playing, when role-playing is viewed as part of a social rather than an exclusively individual system. The two studies presented show that psychiatric and legal screening is typically a peremptory process in which the patient's condition is at best only one of a number of factors which decide the outcome, with social contingencies being of great importance.

The theoretical formulation of symptoms as normative violations places great stress on the social context in which symptomatic behavior occurs, as do the findings concerning the near-automatic procedures in psychiatric screening. Implied in these considerations is a relationship between symptoms, context, and meaning which may be of great importance in future research.

SYMPTOM, CONTEXT, AND MEANING

The admission study showed that involuntary confinement in mental hospitals, in most jurisdictions, is usually based on the presumption of illness by the officials. How accurate is their presumption? The officials whom we interviewed felt that in virtually every case, the family or other complainants sought hospitalization only after exhausting all other alternatives. According to these officials, complainants seek hospitalization only when driven to it by the repeated, meaningless, and uncontrollable behavior of the prospective patient. Prior studies provide support for the belief that some families bend over backwards to avoid hospitalization. Yarrow and others have shown that the defining of repeated rule-breaking as a psychiatric problem is avoided for rather long periods of time.[1]

The officials, then, conceived of the families and other complainants as very reluctant to even consider hospitalization except in cases in which its necessity was a foregone conclusion. Except for some of the court clerks, the officials did not seem to consider the possibility that some of the complainants might have taken action too quickly, rather than too slowly. Are there families in which there is "something wrong" less with the patient, than with the family? In their study of scapegoating in the family, Vogel and Bell found that parental inadequacies and marital conflict were often projected onto

1. M. R. Yarrow et al., "The Psychological Meaning of Mental Illness in the Family." *Journal of Social Issues*, 11 (December, 1955) pp. 12-24.

the weakest child in the family, so that he was "induced" into the role of the deviant.[2] Some empirical evidence for such "induced" roles in complaints about alleged mental illness was found in Philladelphia, where prehospitalization investigation showed that in some 25 per cent of the complaints, it was the complainer, rather than the prospective patient, who was obviously suspect.[3]

The clearest example of the bias of the family's complaints is provided in the work of Laing and Esterson.[4] They present detailed discussions of persons diagnosed as schizophrenics, showing that what is represented to be psychotic symptoms is usually rebellion against extremely tyrannical and bizarre parents. Findings such as theirs have given rise to the belief among many researchers that it is often the families, rather than the patients, who are really "crazy," and that the symptoms of the patients are only normal reactions to very unusual situations.

The formulations concerning "family pathology," although they lead to a more adequate perspective, probably represent only a partial resolution. In his paper on the social dynamics of paranoia, Lemert points out that the complainants who initiate action against a non-conformer may be caught up, with the nonconformer, in a spiral of misinformation, incorrect attributions, and ultimately, in delusions on both sides.[5] According to Lemert's formulation, it is the internal political and social-psychological process of small groups that can lead to ex-

2. E. Vogel and N. Bell, "The Emotionally Disturbed Child as the Family Scapegoat," in N. W. Bell and E. F. Vogel (eds.) *A Modern Introduction to the Family* (London: Routledge & Kegan Paul, 1961), pp. 382-397.
3. Comment by Dr. M. Linden, U. S. Public Health Service, Philadelphia, at the First International Congress of Social Psychiatry, London, August, 1964.
4. R. D. Laing, and A. Esterson, *Sanity, Madness, and the Family* (London: Tavistock Publications) 1964.
5. E. M. Lemert, "Paranoia and the Dynamics of Exclusion," *Sociometry*, 25 (March, 1962), pp. 2-20.

trusion, first informally, and later, formally, from the group. Thus the determinants of extrusion may lie, not in pathology of the complainants, but in the social-psychological situation in the host group, which may generate elementary collective behavior.

Lemert's paper also may serve as a corrective to the view that only the family setting can lead to the kind of nonconforming behavior which is labeled as mental illness. The small groups which Lemert discusses are not in families but in organizations: factions in businesses, factories, and schools. Obviously, however, the faction politics, selective perception, and the attenuation and breakdown of communication between the suspect individual and the rest of the group can occur in families in ways similar to those described by Lemert in large organizations.

Like Laing and Esterson, Lemert indicates that psychiatric symptoms can be understood if seen in the context of the family or group situation in which they occurred. The grave weakness of psychiatric decision-making is the absence of the situational elements. As one psychiatrist has recently pointed out:

A major source of difficulty in psychiatric diagnosis and evaluation is that symptoms are considered to be pathological manifestations *regardless of the context in which they appear. In themselves, however, symptoms are neither normal nor abnormal*: they derive significance only in relation to the [situation in which they occur].[6] [emphasis added]

The refraction that occurs because the context is omitted in psychiatric examinations is nicely documented by Laing and Esterson. With symptom after symptom, they

6. J. V. Coleman, "Social Factors Influencing the Development and Containment of Psychiatric Symptoms," unpublished paper given at the First International Congress of Social Psychiatry, London, August, 1964.

are able to point out how meaningful behavior, when taken out of context, is perceived to be a psychiatric symptom.

To take the first case they discuss, Maya, a 28-year-old mental patient, was diagnosed at 18 years of age as a paranoid schizophrenic, with various symptoms such as auditory hallucinations, ideas of reference and influence, and varying delusions of persecution. Through lengthy and detailed interviews with the patient and her parents, Laing and Esterson were able to put these symptoms in a very different light. By probing into an incident in which the auditory hallucinations were alleged to have occurred, the patient was led to these statements:

She said she had felt quite well at the time: she did not feel that it had to do with her illness. She was responsible for it. She had not been told to act like that by her voices. *The voices, she said, were her own thoughts, anyway.*[7] [emphasis added]

With regard to the alleged ideas of influence, Laing and Esterson found over a year after they began to interview the family, that the father and mother had the idea that Maya could read their thoughts, and that they (the parents) had actually tested her "powers" with experiments in their home. Similarly, the ideas of reference were understandable in context:

An idea of reference that she had was that something she could not fathom was going on between her parents, seemingly about her. Indeed there was. When they were interviewed together, her mother and father kept exchanging with each other a constant series of nods, winks, gestures, knowing smiles, so obvious to the observer, that he commented on them after twenty minutes of the first such interview. They continued, however, unabated and denied.[8]

7. Laing and Esterson, *op. cit.*, p. 25.
8. *Ibid.*, p. 24.

It would appear, then, that the patient's ideas of reference and influence and delusions of persecution were merely descriptions of her parents' behavior towards her. Laing and Esterson document many such misinterpretations in all of the cases they studied.[9]

How do such glaring misinterpretations occur in psychiatric screening? One obvious cause is simple lack of information. Lemert worked for several years in collecting information about eight cases from interviews with relatives, neighbors, physicians, employers, police, attorneys, and jury members. Laing and Esterson spent an average of 25 hours in interviewing each of the 11 families in their study, with a range of from 16 to 50 hours per family. It is obvious that the kind of contextual information which they uncovered could not be collected in an ideal psychiatric interview of one or two hours, much less in the psychiatric interviews we observed in Midwestern State, which took from five to seventeen minutes.

One reason, then, that the behavior of alleged mental patients is thought to be meaningless is that the extremely brief and peremptory psychiatric and judicial interviews shear away most of the information about the context in which the "symptomatic" behavior occurred. There is another kind of factor which leads to the presumption of illness, however, which is more or less independent of the amount of time taken in screening. The medical model, in which nonconforming behavior tends to be seen as a symptom of "mental illness," leads in itself to the ignoring of context.[10] The concept of disease, as it is commonly understood, refers to a process which

9. It should be noted that neither Lemert nor Laing and Esterson *demonstrates* their hypotheses, since their techniques are not rigorously systematic. Their findings, and similar findings by others, however, appear to constitute sufficiently weighty evidence to suggest the need for research that departs radically from conventional psychiatric assumptions.

10. Goffman, *Asylums, op. cit.*

occurs within the body of an individual. Psychiatric symptoms, therefore, are conceived to be a part of a system of behavior which is located entirely within the patient, and which is independent of the social context within which the "symptoms" occur.

It is almost a truism, however, among social psychologists and students of language that the meaning of behavior is not primarily a property of the behavior itself, but of the relation between the bahavior and the context in which it occurs. In his recent paper, Garfinkel has shown how even the most routine and conventional behavior loses its meaning when the penumbra of subtle but multitudinous understandings is omitted.[11] The medical model, since it is based on a conception of physical, rather than social events, fractures the figure-ground relationship between behavior and social context, leading almost inevitably to a bias of seeing suspect behavior as meaningless. Given such a bias, even very extensive and detailed psychiatric interviews would not guarantee against a presumption of illness.

This discussion has suggested that both the theory and practice of psychiatric screening tends to be biased toward seeing behavior of the alleged mentally ill as meaningless, and therefore as symptomatic. The practice of screening, by its brevity, tends to omit contextual information, and the theory, based as it is on the medical model, tends to ignore the contextual information that is available. The remainder of this discussion will be devoted to a brief discussion of some of the implications of these findings for theory and method in the field of abnormal psychology.

Perhaps the clearest implication is the gross unreliability of psychiatric diagnosis as an indication of any-

---

11. H. Garfinkel, "Studies of the Routine Grounds of Everyday Activities," *Social Problems*, 11 (Winter, 1964), pp. 225-250.

thing about the behavior of the mental patient. The process of psychiatric screening would appear to be more sensitive to economic, political and social-psychological pressures on the screening agents than to most aspects of the patient's behavior. This proposition suggests that a basic reorientation is needed in psychological theory and research concerning "mental illness." Too often psychologists and other social scientists simply accept the results of the psychiatric screening process as essentially valid. It is a great convenience to the researcher, after all, to accept society's ready-made measurement of that difficult and elusive dependent variable, psychiatric abnormality, so that he is free to make precise, reliable, and valid measurements of his favorite independent variables. Because of this acceptance, there is now an alarmingly large number of studies which present the ludicrous situation in which there is a refined and sophisticated handling of the independent variable, whether it be genetic, biochemical, psychological, cultural or a host of others; the measurement of "mental illness," however, is left to the obscure, almost unknown vagaries of the process of psychiatric screening.

The acceptance of society's official diagnosis is also convenient for the researcher because it aligns him with the status quo, thus avoiding almost certain conflict with the agencies (such as the hospitals and courts) whose cooperation he needs in order to carry out his research. For the psychologist, it is particularly tempting to accept the societal diagnosis, because most of the common psychological concepts refer to endopsychic processes. Like society, the psychologist may find it much more convenient to locate his concerns in the captive persons of the patients, than in the less easily controlled and investigated processes that occur in the world outside.

To put research into "mental illness" on a scientific basis, and to avoid the situation in which the researcher himself becomes one more arm of the societal reaction to nonconformity, it would seem that the medical model and its attendant psychiatric classifications would need to be eliminated from the program of research. Three areas particularly seem to require such reorientation. Those psychologists who seek the causes of nonconforming behavior should measure their dependent variable behaviorally, and independently of the official societal reaction. Although there have been studies of "mental illness" in which the research has conceptually and operationally defined the dependent variable, the usual pattern is for the study to depend directly or indirectly (as in "known-group" validation) on the societal diagnosis.

A second research area is in the investigation of the micropolitical and social-psychological process of extrusion in small groups such as families, organizational factions, and neighborhood groups. Very little systematic information is now available on the conditions under which extrusion occurs, and on the functions which it fulfills for the group.

A third and final area suggested by this discussion for systematic research is on the dynamics of decision-making in welfare and control agencies. The processes of information transmission, selective perception and agency-client conflict in these agencies have received little attention from scientific investigators. One example of the type of study needed is an investigation of epidemiological differences in rates of mental illness in terms less of the incidence of disease, than in variations in administrative process. A second example of organizational research would concern decision-making in treatment processes. A research project of this type will now be described.

TYPIFICATION IN DIAGNOSIS

In the following discussion I wish to indicate one particular avenue of research that would move outside of the traditional research perspective in rehabilitation. The subject of this discussion is diagnostic, prognostic, and treatment stereotypes of officials and clients and the ways in which these influence treatment processes. Following Sudnow, I will use the generic term, "normal cases." The discussion will begin with a review of Balint's concepts concerning doctor-patient relationships.

One of Balint's conclusions is that there is an apostolic function, i.e., that doctors in some ways function as apostles, seeking to proselytize their patients into having the kinds of diseases that the doctor thinks are conceivable in their cases.[12] It would be easy to accept Balint's statement concerning apostolic mission as academic hyperbole which is used to make a subtle point concerning physical and psychiatric diagnosis. However, one can also take Balint's statement as literally true, and talk about the kinds of organizations and the kinds of situations in which diagnostic stereotypes are used in classifying clientele and become the base for action.

The literal use of such stereotypes is apparent in Sudnow's "Normal Crimes."[13] Making observations in the public defender's office in the court of a large city, he notes that the effective diagnostic unit for the public defender is the *typical* kind of crime: that is, crime typical for this city (the city that he describes) and this

12. M. Balint, *The Doctor, His Patient, and the Illness* (New York: International Universities Press, 1957), p. 216.
13. D. Sudnow, "Normal Crimes: Sociological Features of the Penal Code in a Public Defender's Office," *Social Problems*, 12 (Winter, 1965), pp. 255-276.

time in history. He describes burglary, child molestation, assault with a deadly weapon, and other crimes in terms of the folklore about these crimes that exists in the court in that particular city. To say that this is folklore is not to say that it is completely or even mostly inaccurate. The point that is made, however, is that the thinking of the public defender is in terms of these stereotypic crimes and his questioning of the defendant is not so much an attempt to find the particular dimensions and aspects of the situation in which the defendant finds himself, but almost entirely the extent to which this defendant seems to fit into the stereotyped category of criminal which exists in the court.

I will not attempt to repeat details of this article here. The point that is relevant is that these stereotypes are the functional units which are used by the public defender, and apparently, to a large extent, by the public prosecutor also, in carrying out the business of the court. In this particular case also, it should be noted that the aim of the public defender in using these stereotypes is not so much an attempt to get an acquittal, but a reduction of sentence. This technique is therefore a way of maintaining a smooth-running operation of the court, without gross violation of either the court's concept of punishment, on the one hand, or the defendant's rights, on the other.

It seems likely that such diagnostic stereotypes function in many kinds of treatment, control, and welfare agencies. As the functional units in which business gets done, it is important to note, however, that these diagnostic packages are of different importance in different kinds of organizations and situations. In the kind of situation which one might find, say, in the surgical ward of an outstanding hospital, one would assume that diagnostic stereotypes are used as preliminary hypotheses which are retained or rejected on the basis of further investigation—that is at one pole of the organizational continuum. At the other pole, in the kind of situation which Sudnow describes, these stereotyped are not only first hypotheses but also the final result of the investigation. That is, there is a tendency to accept these stereotyped descriptions with a very minimal attempt to see if they fit the particular case at hand. Later in this discussion I will state some propositions which relate the type of situation, the type of organization, and the functional importance of the diagnostic stereotypes.

The idea of "normal cases" would seem to offer an entering wedge for research in the most diverse kinds of agencies. In current medical practice, the dominant perspective is the "doctrine of specific etiology.[14] This perspective, largely an outgrowth of the successful application of the germ theory of disease, gives rise to the stance of "scientific medicine" in which the conceptual model of disease is a determinate system. The four basic components of this system are a single cause (usually a pathogen in the body), a basic lesion, uniform and invariant symptoms, and regularly recurring outcome, usually damage to the body or death, if medical intervention is not forthcoming.

The model of disease in scientific medicine gives rise to "normal cases" in which diagnosis, prognosis, and treatment are somewhat standardized. (Thus diabetes mellitus is a disease in which the basic lesion is glucose intolerance, primary features are nutritional and metabolic disorders and susceptibility to infection, secondary features are retinopathy, coronary heart disease, renal disease, or neuropathy, and treatment is by routine in-

14. R. Dubos, *Mirage of Health*, (Garden City, N.Y.: Doubleday-Anchor, 1961).

sulin control.) An important component of this disease model is the application for treatment by the patient, with complaints which are traceable to the disease. (Feinstein uses the term "lanthanic" for patients who have the disease but either do not have complaints or whose complaints do not result in application for treatment.)[15] Cases in which the disease is present but the symptoms are not, are obvious deviations from the "normal case" and cause difficulties in medical practice and research. Equally troublesome are causes in which the primary or secondary features of the disease are present, but in which the basic lesion is absent. Meador has suggested, only half in jest, that such conditions be given specific medical status as "nondiseases.[16]

The concept of "normal cases" is closely connected with the notion, in medicine, that physicians have of "What's going around." That is, in a normal practice, a physician is not exposed to all kinds of the most diverse diseases that are described in medical textbooks, but only rather a small sample of diseases, which come in repeatedly: colds, flu, appendicitis, nervous headaches, low back pain, etc.

Proportionately as the case load increases, or inversely as the amount of time that the physician has for each case, as the amount of interest he has, or the amount of knowledge he has, one would expect that these diagnostic stereotypes would play an important role. Some of the atrocity tales of medical practice in armed services or in industry suggest the kinds of eventualities that can occur. For example, at the extreme, in some medical clinics for trainees in the army, virtually all treatments fall into one

15. A. R. Feinstein, "Boolean Algebra and Clinical Taxonomy," *New England Journal of Medicine*, 269 (October 31, 1963), pp. 929-938.

16. C. K. Meador, "The Art and Science of Nondisease," *New England Journal of Medicine*, 272 (January 14, 1965), pp. 92-95.

or two categories—aspirins for headaches and antihista-
mines for colds, and possibly a third category—a talk
with a commanding officer for the residual category of
malingerers.[17]

It is conceivable that the same kinds of conceptual
packages would be used in other kinds of treatment,
welfare and control agencies. Surely in rehabilitation
agencies the conceptual units which the working staff
uses cover only a rather limited number of contingencies
of disability, placement possibilities, and client attitudes.
The same minimal working concepts should be evident in
such diverse areas as probation and parole, divorce cases,
adoption cases, police handling of juveniles, and in the
area of mental health.

Perhaps the most important characteristic of normal
diagnoses, prognoses, and treatments is their validity.
How accurate are the stereotypes which agency workers
and patients use in considering their situations? One
would guess that validity of stereotypes is related to their
precision. Other things being equal, the more precise the
stereotypes, the more ramified they are in the various
characteristics of the client, the situation, and the community, the more accurate one would guess that they
would be. The first proposition, therefore, concerns
simply the number of the different stereotypes that are
used in an agency. One would guess that validity and
precision are correlated. That is, the more numerous the
stereotypes that are actually used in the agency, the
more precise they will be, and the more precise they will
be, the more valid they will be.

Proposition 2 concerns the power of clients. Using the
term "marginality," in the sense used by Krause, the
more marginal the patients the less numerous, precise,

17. Cf. Philip Roth, "Novotny's Pain," *The New Yorker* (October
27, 1962), pp. 46-56.

and valid the stereotypes will be.[18] That is, the more the status of the client is inferior to and different from that of the staff, whether because of economic position, ethnicity, race, education, etc., the more inaccurate and final the normal cases will be.

Proposition 3: The less dependent the agent is upon the client's good will, the less precise and valid the stereotypes will be. In the situation of private practice where the physician is dependent for remuneration upon the patient, one is more likely to find a situation as outlined by Balint, where decision concerning the patient's diagnosis becomes a matter of bargaining.[19] This discussion qualifies Balint's formulation by suggesting that bargaining or negotiation is a characteristic of a medical service in which patients are powerful, such that the diagnostic stereotypes of the physician are confronted by the diagnostic stereotypes of the patient, and that the patient has some power to regulate the final diagnosis.

A fourth proposition relates to the body of knowledge in the agency or profession which is handling the clients. One would suspect that the more substantial or scientific the body of knowledge, the less important, the more valid and the more accurate the conceptual packages. In areas of general medicine, for example, such as pneumonia and syphilis, the kind of stereotyping process discussed here is relatively unimportant. The same would be true in some areas of physical rehabilitation.

A fifth proposition relates the socialization of the staff member to his use of conceptual packages. One would assume that a fairly accurate index of socialization into an agency would be the degree to which a staff member uses the diagnostic packages that are prevalent

18. E. A. Krause, *Factors Related to Length of Mental Hospital Stay*, cited by J. K. Myers in "Consequences and Prognoses of Disability," unpublished paper presented at the Conference on Sociological Theory, Research and Rehabilitation, Carmel, Calif., March, 1965.
19. Balint, *op. cit.*, p. 18.

in that agency. This proposition suggests a final proposition which is somewhat more complicated, relating effectiveness of a staff member in diagnosis or prognosis to his use of diagnostic stereotypes. One would guess that effectiveness has a curvilinear relationship to knowledge and use of stereotypes. In the beginning a new staff member would have only theory and little experience to guide him, and would find that his handling of clients is time-consuming and his diagnoses tend to be inaccurate. As he learns the conceptual packages, he becomes more proficient and more rapid in his work, so that effectiveness increases. The crucial point comes after a point in time in which he has mastered the diagnostic packages and the question becomes, is his perceptiveness of client situations and placement opportunities going to remain at this stereotypic level, where it is certainly more effective than it was when he was a novice in the organization? Is it going to become frozen at this stereotypic level or is he going to go on to begin to use these stereotypes as hypotheses for guiding further investigation on his part? I would suggest that this is a crucial point in the career of any staff member in an agency, and the research which would tell us about this crisis would be most beneficial.[20]

Although carrying out research with normal cases could involve fairly complex procedures (for example, in checking on the validity of diagnostic stereotypes in a series of cases), the beginning efforts in research could be fairly simple. One of the first questions I would want to ask in beginning a study of this kind would be something like, "What kinds of cases do you see most of here in this agency?" With only a little elaboration, I believe

---

20. C. Spaulding has suggested the proposition that typification practices in organizations are also a function of hierarchical position: the higher a person is in the hierarchy (and therefore the more removed from organizational routine) the less stereotyped are his typifications.

such a question would elicit some of the standard stereo-types from most agency staff. Just describing the structure of the normal cases in an agency would be a major step in understanding how that organization functions.

A more ambitious program of research into diagnostic and prognostic treatment stereotypes would be to relate them in each case with the actual outcome of the case. An intermediate stage of research would be represented by any type of gaming study in which experienced, knowledgeable professionals would be assigned simulated cases given information which was found to be the prototypic information used in a given agency. A device for this purpose has been developed by Leslie Wilkins, as found in the appendix of his book on social deviance.[21] Wilkins calls this device an "information board." It contains a large number of items, say 50 items, in which the classification of information from a case history appears on separable index cards with titles of the information appearing on the visible edge of the cards. For example, in the work with probation officers that he did as a pilot study, the information board contained charge, complainant's account of incident, co-defendant's account of incident, offender's account of incident, general appearance of the offender, sex and age of the offender, scholastic attainment, practical handling of problems by the offender, attitudes toward authority, and so on. In the various games that Wilkins had these probation trainees play, he allowed them to select several items from the possible list, and then make a decision. With a little experimentation it should not be difficult to devise diagnostic games with an information board which could be played by the staff of almost any kind of agency.

The two principal kinds of information needed in the proposed research would, first, of the kind of dimensions

21. L. T. Wilkins, *Social Deviance: Social Policy, Action and Research* (Englewood Cliffs, N.J.: Prentice-Hall, 1965), pp. 294-304.

of client condition or behavior which the staff actually uses in its day-to-day decision-making, whether these be blood-pressure, race, continence, attitude toward authority, activity level, prior history of sexual propriety, and so on, and, second, the constellations of values of these dimensions into which the staff (and clients) combine these elements of information into "normal cases."

Conceptually there remain a number of difficulties. In some ways this kind of research is congenial to the approach anthropologists take toward the medical institutions of a small society: the approach to "folk medicine." Anthropological studies of folk medicine seek to describe the medical institutions of a society without accepting the underlying presuppositions of that society. In the same way, the approach to rehabilitation process by way of normal cases seeks to study the flow of business in an organization without accepting the presuppositions of the staff and clients involved. It should be remembered in this connection, however, that in many organizations there are at least two sets of folk involved, staff and clients, each possible having vastly different sets of folk categories of illness or guilt, etc.

From the point of view of orderly conceptual formulation, none of the concepts used in this discussion (e.g., diagnostic stereotypes, normal cases, and conceptual packages) are particularly satisfactory. The concept of stereotypes implies more distortion than is intended, and does not articulate very well with organizational structure.[22] Normal cases is a good enough general term, but does not lead to a more detailed breakdown of sub-elements.[23] Conceptual packages is much too general a term. Perhaps the best set of concepts would be taken

22. D. Zimmerman called my attention to Schutz's term, "typifications."

23. M. Loeb has suggested to me that "standard cases" would be preferable terminology.

from role analysis. Normal cases imply a set of role expectations which articulate with the position of the perceiver in the organization. Diagnostic stereotypes in medicine, for example, might be construed as the counterrole variants that make up the physicians' role-set for patients. The concept of role seems somewhat static for this use, and does not immediately suggest conceptual analogies for prognostic (role-futures?) or treatment stereotypes. Perhaps some of these difficulties can be removed through further discussion.

One way of conceptualizing the problem in a broader context is in terms of the *work system* in organizations. Often there is considerable difference between the official version of the work done in an organization and what actually gets done. The discussion above suggests that there may be a relatively small number of dimensions which determine the actual work system: the typifications described above, the consensus on work rates (suggested by Howard Becker) and the precision and dependability with which work output is measured, for example. These dimensions provide the bare suggestions that the culture of the workplace may be considered to be an over-determined, self-maintaining system, and should therefore be studied as an analytical whole.

The purpose of these comments has been to formulate the kind of research which would avoid the undue emphasis on the individual and the physical, as well as other presuppositions of the professionals who specialize in the rehabilitation process. This difference of viewpoint from those used in the agencies would likely cause some practical difficulties in carrying out research of this kind. Difficulties of a methodological and conceptual character have already been alluded to above. Nevertheless, the program of research suggested here might provide a useful approach to a large number of problems in rehabilitation and medical organizations.

MENTAL ILLNESS AND SOCIAL STATUS

It would appear that the looseness of psychiatric theory and procedures, interacting with the attitudes of persons in the community, welfare, and control agencies, gives rise to a situation in which individualistic concepts, whether medical or psychological, can explain only part of the variation in the handling of the mentally ill. It has been suggested here that the serious student of regularities in our society may find it profitable to study "mental illness" in terms of "career contingencies," (as in the study of decision-making in the release of mental patients from mental hospitals in Chapter 5) which governs passage between the status of the ordinary citizen and that of the mental patient.

Sociologically, a status is defined as a set of rights and duties. Although we tend to take the rights and duties of the ordinary citizen for granted, it becomes clear that there is an extensive set of rights and duties which define the status of the sane, when we realize the rights which are abridged when a person is declared mentally incompetent, i.e., roughly speaking, when he is committed to a mental hospital. The following is a partial list of such rights:

TABLE 8

LEGAL AREAS INVOLVING COMPETENCY

1. Making a will (testamentary capacity)
2. Making a contract deed, sale
3. Being responsible for a criminal act
4. Standing trial for a criminal charge
5. Being punished for a criminal act
6. Being married
7. Being divorced

8. Adopting a child
9. Being a fit parent
10. Suing and being sued
11. Receiving property
12. Holding property
13. Making a gift
14. Having a guardian, committee or trustees
15. Being committed to a mental institution
16. Being discharged from a mental institution
17. Being paroled or put on probation
18. Being responsible for a tortious civil wrong
19. Being fit for military service
20. Being subject to discharge from the military service
21. Operating a vehicle
22. Giving a valid consent
23. Giving a binding release or waiver
24. Voting
25. Being a witness (testimonial capacity)
26. Being a judge or juror
27. Acting in a professional capacity, as a lawyer, teacher, physician
28. Acting in a public representative capacity, as a governor, legislator
29. Acting in a fiduciary capacity, as trustee, executor
30. Managing or participating in a business, as a director, stockholder
31. Receiving compensation for inability to work as a result of an injury.[24]

It should be understood that this list includes only those rights that are formally and officially lost and does not include rights that may be informally abrogated, either during or after hospitalization. Such a collection of abro-

24. R. R. Mezer and P. D. Rheingold, "Mental Capacity and Incompetency: A Psycho-Legal Problem," *American Journal of Psychiatry*, 118 (1962), pp. 827-831.

gated rights points out that there is a distinct and separate status for the mentally ill in our society.

Throughout this report there have been instances in which the mental patient has been compared with other disadvantaged persons of low social status. In this final section, it will be argued that it is helpful to make a formal statement in which discussions of mental illness are translated to the language of social role and status; the social institution of insanity can be considered to be constituted by a "status line" between persons designated as sane and those designated to be mentally ill.

Most sociological concepts which have been developed to describe status lines refer to the norms which govern contact between races: the "color line." The structure of a color line, as formulated by Strong, and others, is built up around two statuses, the status of the ingroup member, and that of the outgroup member.[25] Between these two statuses is the category of exception, for persons assigned to neither group. Finally, completing the axis of statuses, is the status ideal, which embodies the values of the ingroup, and the negative status ideal, which embodies the vices. That is, the status ideals portray the ingroup hero and villain, respectively. Corresponding to each of the five statuses is the appropriate role, which specifies the characteristics of persons occupying the status.

Applied to the status line which separates deviants and non-deviants, this axis would contain the ideal status, or hero of conformity to ingroup values, the conventional conforming role, the categories of exception, which have

25. S. M. Strong, "Social Types in a Minority Group," *American Journal of Sociology*, 48 (March, 1943), pp. 563-573. For an application to deviance of concepts drawn from race relations, see Goffman in a section of "Some Dimensions of the Problem," in Milton Greenblatt, D. J. Levinson, and R. H. Williams (eds.), *The Patient and the Mental Hospital*, (Glencoe, Ill.: Free Press, 1957) p. 508.

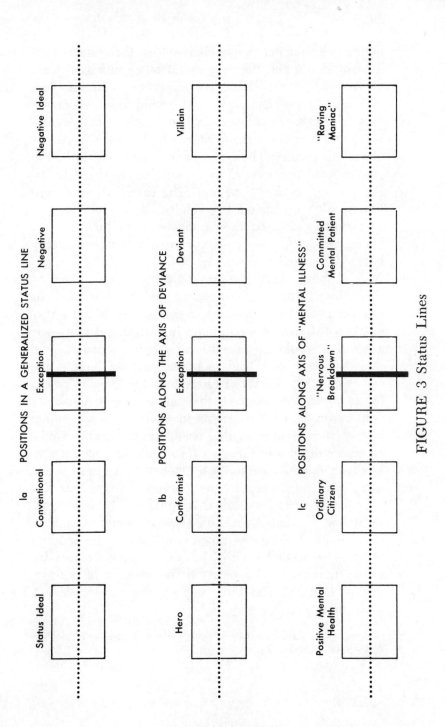

Ia POSITIONS IN A GENERALIZED STATUS LINE

Status Ideal   Conventional   Exception   Negative   Negative Ideal

Ib POSITIONS ALONG THE AXIS OF DEVIANCE

Hero   Conformist   Exception   Deviant   Villain

Ic POSITIONS ALONG AXIS OF "MENTAL ILLNESS"

Positive Mental   Ordinary   "Nervous   Committed   "Raving
Health   Citizen   Breakdown"   Mental Patient   Maniac"

FIGURE 3 Status Lines

neither deviant nor non-deviant status, the conventional deviant status, and the negative ideal, or super-villain.

Applied to the status separation between the sane and insane, the negative ideal would be the "raving lunatic" of heroic proportions, and other such stereotypes which embody the most intense fears and aversions of the community. The status of the insane would be the conventional negative status, being roughly the status of the committed mental patient. The categories of exception would correspond to such conditions as "nervous breakdown," as used as a euphemism in popular parlance, and "temporary insanity," in which a person's behavior is excused without penalty.

The conventional conforming status would be that of the ordinary citizen whose sanity has not been called in question. What corresponds, in our society to the status ideal on this axis of separation? In earlier societies, such a question would have been less difficult to answer, since most societies have held unambiguous and largely uncontested images of the virtuous man. In medieval Japan, for example, the image of the samurai would undoubtedly correspond to the status ideal. In our own earlier history, the members of the "elect," predestined to God's grace, would also fit this status. In contemporary society, however, religious authority no longer serves to give unquestioned legitimacy to the positive virtues, and the formulation of the role ideal is continuously in process.

It may be that the nearest that our society comes to a status ideal along the sane-insane axis is the concept of "positive mental health." Jahoda reports no consensus among psychological experts on the criterion of positive mental health.[26] The following six criteria are among those most prominent:

26. M. Jahoda, *Current Concepts of Positive Mental Health* (New York: Basic Books, 1958).

1. Attitudes toward one's self: self-esteem, correctness of self-conception, etc.
2. Growth, development, or self-actualization
3. Integration of the self
4. Autonomy; independence
5. Adequacy of perception of reality
6. Mastery of the environment

These disparate and conflicting criteria of mental health would appear to be little related to ordinary notions of health, but rather formulations of what the various authors regard to be the highest values to which our society ought to aspire in shaping ourselves and our children.[27] As such values, the concept of "positive mental health" comes very close to being what has been described as the status ideal.

Wallace's biocultural model of mental illness bears some resemblance to this model of the status line.[28] Wallace describes five *states* which make up the "theory" of mental illness held by the members of a society: Normalcy (*N*), Upset (*U*), Psychosis (*P*), In Treatment (*T*), and Innovative Personality (*I*). The sequences of states are presented in the following diagram:

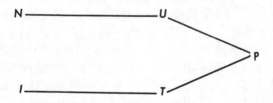

27. M. B. Smith, "Mental Health Reconsidered: A Special Case of the Problem of Values in Psychology," *American Psychologist*, 16 (1961), pp. 299-306.

28. A. F. C. Wallace, "Mental Illness, Biology, and Culture," in Francis L. K. Hsu (ed.), *Psychological Anthropology* (Homewood, Ill.: Dorsey Press, 1961), pp. 255-295.

In the case where the Innovative Personality is equiva-
lent to Normalcy, the diagram becomes:

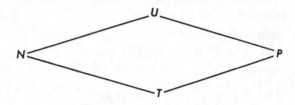

In this version, N corresponds to the conventional status,
and P to the deviant status, with U and T representing
the unlabeled and labeled phases of primary rule-breaking, respectively. Both of these phases fall on or near the
status line that separates the in-group and out-group.

There is one way in which the Wallace model is
fundamentally different than the one presented here,
however. His model is based on *beliefs* of members of
the society, their "theories" of behavior, and is not directly connected with actual behavior. In the model of
the status system discussed here, the positions in the
system are actual social positions, each comprised by a
set of rights and duties, each recognized as legitimate
social entities by the members of the society. Corresponding to the transfer mechanisms that Wallace posits (the
mechanisms that explain to the satisfaction of the members of the society how the sick person moves from
one state to another) in the present model would be the
actual social procedures, the *rites de passage* which ac-
complish the transfer of the person from one status to
another. Thus Wallace's model complements the social
system model, since it concerns the individual beliefs
which accompany behavior. It would appear that both
of the models are necessary to describe the system of
behavior involved in the recognition and treatment of
mental illness.

One of the most important characteristics of any

status system is its permeability, i.e., the ease or difficulty of passage from one status to another. A status system which is impermeable is called a caste system; status systems which are permeable may be called class systems. Many of the reform programs that have been carried on in the last several decades in the mass media, and more recently, in the mental hospitals, have been attempts to make the system more permeable, to desegregate first and then, after desegregation, to democratize the status of the mentally ill.

Needless to say, these programs have met with some outstanding successes; it is undoubtedly true that the typical mental patient today has much better chance of passing back into his nondeviant status than he would have fifty or even twenty-five years ago. It is also true, however, that the status system of insanity still has caste-like aspects, as can be still seen on the back wards of most mental hospitals, as well as in many other ways. It is also true that increasing permeability in such a status system means not only that those in the status of the insane can pass more easily into the sane status, but also that those in the sane status can pass more easily into that of the insane. It has been frequently remarked by planners or mental health services that such services appear to be bottomless pits; the more that are provided, the more demand there seems to be.

An interesting, if somewhat unfortunate, consequence of the fact that social attitudes play such a big role in the definition of mental illness is that mental health education may be a two-edged sword. By teaching people to regard certain types of distress or behavioral oddities as illnesses rather than as normal reactions to life's stresses, harmless eccentricities, or moral weaknesses, it may cause alarm and increase the demand for psychotherapy. This may explain the curious fact that the use of psychotherapy tends to keep pace with its availability. The greater the number of treatment facilities and the more widely they are known, the larger the number of persons seeking their help. Psychotherapy is the only form of treatment which, at least to some extent, appears to create the illness it treats.[29]

Increasing permeability could also mean, as Szasz has suggested, simply that more diverse kinds of problems, welfare, moral, political, are being funnelled into psychiatric channels. In a thoughtful review of what he calls the "inflationary demand" for psychiatric services, Schofield makes the following observation:

It is time for the leaders of the mental health movement to put their minds to . . . analysis of problems which psychiatry and psychology have tended to neglect: to criteria of mental health, to delimitation of the meanings and forms of mental illness, to specification of precisely what are and what are not *psychiatric* problems. It would be a positive contribution for mental health educators to develop ways of communicating to the public on such questions as: "When not to go to the psychiatrist"; or "What to do before you see a psychiatrist"; "What psychotherapy cannot do for you"; "Ten sources of helpful conversations"; "Problems which do not make you a 'Mental Case.' "[30]

Both Frank and Schofield seem to be counseling the need for denial, in the face of the tendencies toward routine labeling in the ideology of the mental health movement.

These considerations pose policy problems, which, as such, are not the main focus of this discussion. We have sought in this book to provide a framework which would allow for a disciplined description of the way in which persons deemed mentally ill are handled in our society. It is not intended that this framework be accepted as a precise description of the social system which

29. J. D. Frank, *Persuasion and Healing* (Baltimore: The Johns Hopkins Press, 1961), pp. 6-7.
30. W. Schofield, *Psychotherapy: The Purchase of Friendship* (Englewood Cliffs, N.J.: Prentice-Hall, 1964), p. 147.

is operative in mental illness precesses, but only as a step toward more adequate theory and research. Such a framework may prove useful not only in research on mental illness, but also in related areas of deviant behavior, such as crime and mental retardation. As has been mentioned before, race relations also would seem to have structures and dynamics similar to those outlined here.

One field, finally, that deserves mention in this connection is international relations. Perry, in his formulation of "the role of the national," has begun the kind of conceptualization of the status dynamics between nations that has been discussed here for mental illness.[31] Such formulations are badly needed in many areas of social science, since they promise to provide a bridge between social and individual processes. The integration of these two areas of research remains one of the principle tasks of social science. The theory presented here is intended as a step toward such integration.

FINAL COMMENT

This book has outlined an approach to the study of mental illness which takes the motive forces out of the individual patient and puts them into the system constituted by the patient, other persons reacting to him, and the official agencies of control and treatment in the society. The theory, and the evidence relevant to the truth or falsity of the theory, are presented in the first part of the book. Acknowledging that the evidence was far from complete, both in amount and quality, the author concluded that the existing state of evidence favored this sociological theory, perhaps only slightly, relative to the alternative traditional theory based on the

31. S. E. Perry, "Notes on the Role of the National," *Conflict Resolution*, 1 (December, 1957), pp. 346-363.

individual system model. Obviously the author is pre-
disposed to accept the theory, and may not have been
sufficiently impartial in his selection and evaluation of
the evidence. Other investigators, more objective than
the author, might review the state of evidence and come
to a contrary conclusion. Perhaps it might be worth-
while if such a review were made, independently, assessing the state of evidence with respect to each of the
propositions in Part I.

The same point might be made with respect to Part II,
the studies of decision-making in general medicine and
psychiatry. Studies similar to these might be repeated,
in different settings by independent investigators, to
assess the validity and generality of the results reported
here. Both the review of the state of evidence, and the
field studies repeating those reported here, would likely
be contributions to the developing sociology of mental
illness.

A more valuable contribution might be made, however, if instead of seeking to repeat the assessment of
the literature, or the field studies reported here, other
researchers sought to modify and refine the theory and
research techniques discussed here. The propositions in
Part I, at their best, are very crude statements, lacking
specificity and rigor. As Buckley notes in his methodological note (in the Appendix), the nine propositions
discussed represent a somewhat arbitrary selection from
a larger number of propositions implicit in the theory.
This theory, it would seem, should serve as a starting
point for the development of a more complete and coherent set of propositions. This set, in turn, could lead
to better research, and further our understanding, both
of mental illness, and of social processes which regulate
conformity and deviance.

In future research informed by this theory, it would
be desirable to increase not only the specificity but also

the scope of the investigation. A large-scale study which tested many of the propositions simultaneously can easily be envisioned. One such study, for example, would be a longitudinal field study of residual rule-breakers which used an experimental design. In such a study, a survey would be used to locate rule-breakers who have not been labeled in the community. The rule-breakers would be divided into groups according to the amount and degree of their violations, with perhaps one group who repeatedly violate fundamental rules, at one extreme, and at the other, a group of persons who infrequently violate less important rules. Whatever the number and composition of these groups, each would be further divided at random into a labeled group and "denial" group. That is, the rule-breakers in the labeled group would be exposed to the normal processes of recognition, definition, and treatment as mentally ill, and the denial group would be shielded from such processes. The effects of the labeling and denial could then be systematically assessed over a period of time.

To carry out such a study properly, even with a relatively small sample of rule-breakers, would require rather large amounts of money, time, and ingenuity. It would involve some taxing and delicate problems of ethics in research, and of the responsibility of the researcher to his subjects and to the community. Nevertheless, if the position discussed here has any validity, if only in small part, the results of such a study could be enormously revealing. The likely conclusion of such a study would not be a clear verification or falsification of this theory, but of indications of the conditions under which the social system determines case outcomes: the type of rule-breaker, community, psychiatric or other treatment, and situation in which the social system theory gives a fairly accurate picture of the sequence of events.

Future research aside, how successfully has the present discussion met its proposed tasks: to formulate a purely sociological theory of chronic mental illness, to compare this theory with current alternative theories, and to judge the relative worth of these competing theories? Some shortcomings are obvious. The exclusion of the personal characteristics of the rule-breaker from the analysis, for example, probably limits the predictive power of the theory. To take just one characteristic: if there is a general trait of suggestibility, as is sometimes argued, this trait would figure prominently in the process of entering or not entering the role of the mentally ill. Contrary to the assumption made here, rule-breakers do vary in their personal characteristics: some have intensely held convictions, some do not; some are sophisticated about legal and medical procedures, and others are not; some are deferential to authority, and so on. These characteristics are probably important in determining how resistant a rule-breaker will be to entering the deviant role when it is offered. Many other dimensions which would qualify and augment the theory could also be pointed out.

As was noted in the first chapter, however, the purpose of this discussion was not that of final explanation, but of a starting point for systematic analysis. To evaluate the usefulness of the theory, the reader must ask two questions: how convincing is the analysis of careers of mental illness, which uses gross social processes such as denial and labeling, rather than the intricate intra-psychic mechanisms postulated in the medical model? Secondly, to what extent does the "clash of doctrines," to use Whitehead's phrase, which is developed here, illuminate the current controversy over policy, theory, and research in the area of mental illness? A definitive answer to these questions may be provided by future research. For the present, the reader must be guided by his own inclination and judgment.

COMPARED to most "theories" in sociology—which are usually more adequately describable as conceptual or categorical frameworks—this theory of stable mental disorder has the rare merit of looking like a theory. Viewed in the stark light of its explicit propositional form, it becomes easy to understand why there are so few of this nature: not only are they more easily subject to empirical test, but they invite immediate critical comment.

The diagram, or flow chart (see page 100, Chapter 3) was originally drawn as an aid to visualizing the theory as a whole and the way the various propositions were interrelated with one another. But this led to an interest in (1) the nature and source of the propositions themselves, and (2) the "causal texture," so to speak, of the theory.

(1) It became clear that in order to complete or bring closure to a reasonable flow diagram of the theory, it was necessary to augment Scheff's specifically labeled propositions or variables with others taken from the textual material. In other words, the labeling of propositions and basic variables was arbitrary relative to other statements and variables in the text equally warranting the status of propositions or formal concepts in a more finished theory. This is indicated in the diagram by assigning numbers above to the original explicit propositions

201

(such as No. 1, No. 2, etc.) and adding auxiliary propositions (as 8a, 8b, etc.) that were implicit in the text. This means, among other things, that the reader was forced to build some of the formal theory as he went along, thus, needless to say, introducing another source of arbitrariness and possible misunderstanding.

One lesson here, then, is that each theorist would do well to develop a flow diagram for any theory he may create. For a flow diagram—product of the modern age of computers and cybernetic systems—can be seen as a device of the "new" mathematics and systems research that can represent the logical structure of a system, whether a substantive or a conceptual system. Hence, even in a very simple form it can be extremely useful in explicating or exposing a loosely verbalized theory.[1] Viewing one's theory in diagramatic form invites the theorist to ask such questions as these: Which statements are to be taken as axiomatically assumed, which are definitions, which are hypotheses, which have a great deal of empirical support, etc. It also makes more obvious, sometimes painfully so, any gaps in the theoretical structure, or suggests that the theory remains too indeterminate without further specification of the conditions under which propositions or hypotheses may be expected to hold. And then there is the question whether the presumed theory can be diagramed at all—which may be a question of whether the theory has any logical structure, i.e., whether it is a theory after all.

(2) If a theory is complex, some kind of diagram may be essential to bring out the "causal flow." This is of central importance today as more and more sociological theories take seriously the transactional or *systemic* nature of the phenomena they are attempting to explain.

1. See, for example, J. G. March and H. A. Simon, *Organizations* (New York: Wiley, 1958).

Methodological orientations used to inform most theories may perhaps be classified into four main types. The traditional causal perspective appeals to one or more prior elements of a complex of factors as leading to the phenomenon being explained. Recent examples are the "funnel of causation" orientation of Angus Campbell, *et al.*, in *The American Voter*,[2] and Neil Smelser's "value-added" approach in his *Theory of Collective Behavior*.[3] Functionalism attempts to work in the opposite direction, seeking to explain a phenomenon in terms of its effects on the complex of which it is a part. Equilibrium system theory, focusing on a mutual interactionism, denies cause and effect distinctions and sees only reciprocal interrelations. The work of Pareto and early Homans are good examples. But this orientation is of use only for closed systems, having little application to open systems characterized by adaptation, restructuring, elaboration, or evolution. Finally, the modern systems research approach focuses on open systems of organized complexity, which have a history, are morphogenic, and hence continuously elaborate, develop, or degenerate depending on the dynamic structure of interrelations of the parts among themselves and with environmental events.[4] The main concern is to study the various types of complex interrelations of parts or mechanisms that have developed from earlier states and which are elaborating or degenerating in some specifiable ways.

Theories of social deviance can be seen to have run the gamut of these orientations. Earlier simple causal theories, *e.g.*, of the "bad seed" type have given way

2. A. Campbell *et al.*, *The American Voter* (New York: Wiley, 1960).
3. N. J. Smelser, *Theory of Collective Behavior* (New York: Free Press, 1963).
4. In a forthcoming book to be published by Prentice-Hall, I indicate some of the important implications of systems research for sociological theory.

to more complex causal theories involving earlier social environment and acquired psychological traits as major antecedent factors. Equilibrium theory sees deviance as embedded in a matrix of reciprocal interrelations of elements, such that, after Homans, any departure from the existing degree of conformity to (or deviance from) the group norms is automatically counteracted by equilibrial forces to restore that degree—that is, if the system is a closed one in equilibrium. Functionalism has always had a bit of trouble over the problem of deviance: since deviance is usually seen as extrasystemic and primarily dysfunctional, its universality of persistence cannot very well be explained in terms of the usual functional attributions. Most usually the functionalist shifts gears to an equilibrium and appeals to automatic "mechanisms of control" to handle the disturbing deviance.

As I see it, the theory of deviance that is emerging today—of which Scheff's work is a contribution—is in the spirit of the modern systems approach. This theory sees deviance as a system product, one generated out of a complex network of events involving: the historically generated institutional and cultural structure with its vested interests and "moral entrepreneurs"; the matrix of interpersonal transactions within this structure whereby the strains of everyday role-playing generate adjustments, bargainings, and random or trial deviations which, in a context of "societal reactions," may lead to a "labeling" of the self as deviant; the resultant build-up of career deviants—whether aggregates of the mentally ill, subcultures of the alienated, or formal organizations of criminals; and the reactions of these groups directly and indirectly back onto the institutional structure to contribute to its continual elaboration or disintegration. It would seem that any theory that begins to get at the intricacies involved here will have to make use of some kind of tool like the flow-diagram to keep track of what it is saying and what it implies, to reveal the multiple interconnections and the positive and negative feedbacks so necessary to an understanding of process, or structural dynamics in complex open systems. Thus, the flow diagram in this volume (page 100, Chapter 3), though only illustrative, suggests some of the intricacies, including possible feedback loops, implied or invited by that theory.

Finally, as theories come to take account of the systemic nature of social phenomena, methodologists concerned with logical implications and empirical tests will have to upgrade their canons of acceptance. It is no longer enough to focus on pairs or trios of interrelated variables and test for correlations. For a theory may be wrong, even though the separate propositions check out, because the variables are not interrelated into the correct overall structure.

Name Index

Ames, L. B., 52
Andersen, R. M., 121
Angrist, S., 97
Apter, N. S., 9
Arieti, S., 8, 61

Bakwin, H., 112
Balint, M., 52, 85, 116, 118, 178, 183
Baum, G. L., 53, 118
Beck, A. T., 161
Becker, H., 2, 32-33, 93
Bell, N., 171
Bellak, L., 7
Bendit, D., 95
Benedict, R., 93-94
Benjamins, J., 57
Bennett, A. M. H., 43
Bennett, C. C., 41
Berne, E., 17-19
Blake, R. R., 63
Blau, Z. S., 57
Brauchi, J. T., 42
Brill, H., 72
Broom, L., 57, 129
Brown, E. L., 133
Buckley, W., 99, 201 ff.
Bushard, B. L., 152

Cain, A. C., 67
Campbell, A., 203
Caudill, W., 85
Chassan, J. B., 57
Chernoff, H., 124
Clausen, J. A., 47, 115
Cohen, L. H., 72
Coleman, J. V., 172

Culver, D. M., 130
Cummings, E., 47, 48, 154
Cummings, J., 47, 48, 154

Darley, W., 114
Davis, J. A., 156
Dawber, T. R., 115, 116
Dinitz, S., 97, 156
Dubos, R., 180
Dunn, J. P., 115

Ehrlich, J., 127
Eichorn, R. L., 121
Ellis, A., 57
Erikson, K. T., 17, 88, 152
Esterson, A., 17, 171, 173, 174
Etter, L. E., 115
Eysenck, H. J., 152

Feinstein, A. R., 181
Fenichel, O., 10-11
Fenwick, M., 38
Fogelson, R. D., 24
Frank, J. D., 196
Freeman, H., 72
Freeman, J. E., 156
Freud, S., 10-14

Gainford, J., 167
Gardiner-Hill, H., 120
Garfinkel, H., 81, 175
Garland, L. H., 111, 112
Ginzberg, E., 83
Glass, A. J., 52, 83, 120, 152
Goffman, E., 17, 34-38, 81, 97, 121, 155, 174, 190
Gordon, J. E., 48, 115, 151

207

Hagstrom, W. O., 73
Hastings, D. W., 72
Hayward, M. L., 62
Herbert, C. C., 83
Heron, W., 42
Hill, A. B., 117
Hollingshead, A. B., 47, 49, 88-90, 98, 127

Ilg, F. L., 52

Jackson, P. D., 7, 8
Jahoda, M., 191

Kardiner, A., 52
Kellam, S. G., 57
Keys, A., 115
Kinsey, A. C., 115
Kitsuse, J., 128
Klapp, O. E., 57
Koos, E. L., 97
Korvonen, M. J., 115
Krasner, L., 19-22
Kraus, E. A., 183
Kuhn, T., 27
Kutner, L., 133

Laing, R. D., 17, 171, 173, 174
Ledley, R. S., 124-25
Lefton, M., 97
Leighton, D. C., 48
Lemert, E. M., 17, 51, 60, 87, 97, 116, 118, 155, 171, 174
Lewis, N. D. C., 7
Lieberman, S., 57
Linden, M., 171
Linn, E. L., 156
Loeb, M., 186
Lowenthal, M. F., 134
Lusted, L. B., 124-25

Malzberg, B., 72
Mann, G. V., 116
Mann, J. H., 57
March, J. G., 202
Martin, C. E., 115
Marx, K., 14-17
Meador, C. K., 181
Mechanic, D., 26, 97, 132
Meth, J. M., 61

Mezer, R. R., 184
Middleton, R., 76
Miller, D., 133
Mishler, E. G., 134
Moland, J., 76
Moore, F. E., 116
Morehead, M., 127
Moses, L. E., 124
Mouton, J. S., 63
Myers, J. D., 183

Neyman, J., 108, 110
Nunnally, J. C., 68-70, 78

Parsons, T., 118
Pasamanick, B., 49-50, 97
Perry, S. E., 197
Phillips, D. L., 87
Plunkett, R. J., 48, 115, 151
Pokorny, A. D., 73
Pomeroy, W. B., 115
Porterfield, A. L., 115
Pronko, N. H., 1

Rappeport, J. R., 72
Ratner, H., 114
Rautaharju, P. M., 115
Redlich, F. C., 47, 49, 127
Rheingold, P. D., 184
Rogler, L. H., 88-90, 98
Rosenzweig, N., 46
Ross, H. A., 131, 153, 160
Roth, P., 182

Sadow, L., 59-60
Saunders, L., 83
Schacter, S., 63
Scheff, T. J., 135
Schofield, W., 196
Schwartz, J., 53, 118
Scott, W. A., 46
Selznick, P., 57, 129
Shibutani, T., 91
Simmons, O. G., 156
Simon, H. A., 202
Singer, J. E., 63
Smelser, N. J., 203
Smith, M. B., 193
Spaulding, C., 184
Spencer, K., 156